The
WILD
MUSHROOM
COOKBOOK

Joy O. I. Spoczynska

Illustrated by Kenneth H. Poole

GREEN
PRINT

First published in 1991 by
Green Print
an imprint of the Merlin Press
10 Malden Road, London NW5 3HR

© Joy O. I. Spoczynska (text)
© Kenneth H. Poole (illustrations)
The right of Joy O. I. Spoczynska to be identified as author of this work has been
asserted in accordance with the Copyright, Design and Patents Act 1988.

ISBN 1 85425 062 0

Phototypeset by Computerset Ltd., Harmondsworth, Middlesex

Printed in England by Biddles Ltd., Guildford, Surrey
on recycled paper

The
WILD
MUSHROOM
COOKBOOK

8.20

Please note . . .

● It is essential that any wild fungus gathered for eating should be correctly identified. The information and illustrations in this book are intended to assist with identification, but are *not a substitute* for a detailed botanical guide. Neither the author nor the publishers of this book can be held responsible for the incorrect identification of a fungus, and suitable reference books are listed on page 116.

● Some of the recipes in this book reflect traditional country recipes and use meat. If you eat meat we urge you to ensure that it is from organically fed and humanely slaughtered animals. Advice on suitable suppliers in your area can be obtained from the Soil Association, 86 Colston Street, Bristol B51 5BB (telephone 0272 290661).

Contents

ACKNOWLEDGEMENTS

I wish to acknowledge my thanks for permission granted by Messrs. Robert Hale Ltd., the publishers of my book *The Wildfoods Cookbook*, to reproduce some of the recipes originally published in the Mushroom section of that book.

I also wish to thank the following individuals who contributed some of the recipes: Laura Kroy, Maria van Booys and Neltje Kaufman of the Mennonite Community in Akron, Ohio, USA; Deborah Turner of the Wooden Shoe Commune, also in Ohio; Dorothy Cierpiala of New York City; Lotte Heidemann of Düsseldorf, Germany; and Marietta Arends of Jönköping, Sweden.

I would also like to record my thanks to my secretary, Marion Bishop, who made such a good job of typing the draft from tape.

Finally, my thanks are due to my illustrator, Kenneth H. Poole, who kindly provided all the line drawings – no light undertaking!

J.O.I.S.

Part 1: WILD MUSHROOMS

An introduction to fungi

More than a hundred good edible species of mushrooms grow in the British Isles alone, and the important thing is to know whether a species is edible or not. It is essential to be able to recognise it infallibly and to discard any specimen of whose identity you are not certain. Several edible species have very distinctive features and cannot possibly be confused with any others; on the other hand, there are edible species which have somewhat similar-looking counterparts among the inedible kinds, and one or two of them are not unlike certain very poisonous species. The best course for the beginner to adopt is to learn to *know* them: to know the edible species without any possibility of error and to know the ones to avoid.

The properties of fungi

Fungi differ botanically from other plants so completely that it is necessary to say a little about their nature before going on to describe the various species.

Fungi, like mosses, ferns, lichens and seaweeds, are flowerless plants. They do not produce seeds, but propagate themselves by means of spores, minute bodies no larger than microscopic particles of dust, which together look like a fine powder. These spores vary in colour, usually according to the sub-group to which the mushroom belongs. The colour of the spores is in many cases a diagnostic feature; once you are sure of the sub-group, this will help you to identify the species by a process of elimination. Enormous quantities of spores are produced; since they are so minute, vast numbers of them are wasted.

Producing spores instead of seeds is not the only difference between fungi and other plants. They do not possess chlorophyll, the green colouring matter in flowering plants, ferns and mosses, and this is the reason for their completely different method of obtaining nutrition. While green plants utilise air, water and sunlight to form nutrient materials with chlorophyll acting as a catalyst, fungi, on the other hand, live on organic matter, either living or dead, from which they absorb their food ready-made, as it were. Those which derive their nourishment from living animals or plants are called parasites, and usually cause disease in their hosts; an example is the rust fungus of wheat. Those which grow on dead organic matter are known as saprophytes; these include such fungi as the timber-infesting wet rot and dry rot fungi and also the vast majority of the large fleshy fungi with which this book is concerned.

Each mushroom consists of two parts, one visible and one which develops underground. This latter part is the vegetative portion, which serves the nutrition of the individual mushroom; the visible part above ground is the reproductive portion which is, of course, concerned with the perpetuation of the species – in other words, the production of spores.

A system of finely-branched threads grows on the wood, leaf-mould, soil or other substance on which the fungus is found. These threads, through which nutrients are absorbed, are analogous to the roots in flowering plants and are called the mycelium. The visible part of the fungus is called the fruit-body; this fruit-body is the edible part for our purposes, and is the important part to be described for recognition.

The large, fleshy fungi are classified into two main groups. The first group is the Ascomycetes, in which the spores develop inside minute sacs; the truffles belong to this group. The other group, to which the vast majority of mushrooms belong, is known as the Basidiomycetes, in which the spores develop at the tips of small club-shaped organs forming a layer in or on the fruit-body. Basidiomycetes are divided into two smaller sub-groups. In one of these the spores develop inside a closed fruit-body and are set free either through an opening to the exterior or by means of disintegration of the walls of the fruit-body; the puffballs belong to this group. In the other sub-group spores are formed on surfaces open to the air so that they can be windborne as soon as they have matured. The common cultivated mushroom is a familiar example of the latter group, which is sub-divided into various families according to the form of the spore-bearing surface, which may consist of plate-like gills, tubes, spines or smooth surfaces.

The structure of fungi

The largest group of edible mushrooms is the gill fungi or agarics. Since it is essential to know the different parts of the fungus which serve as diagnostic features, some of these characteristics are shown in Fig. 1. These will now be separately described.

Universal veil

A young unexpanded mushroom is frequently enclosed in an unbroken membrane known as the universal veil, though in a few species this veil is absent. As the fungus grows the veil, which does not keep pace with it, ruptures. In a few genera a thin membrane connects the edge of the cap with the stem; this is known as the secondary veil, which covers and protects the gills in the immature stage. As the cap expands this secondary veil becomes detached from the edge of the cap, forming a ring round the stem (in those agarics which have no secondary or universal veil there is no ring). Sometimes fragments of the detached secondary veil remain on the upper surface of the cap forming rough patches.

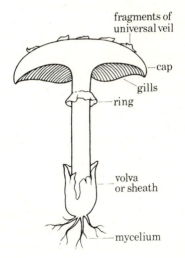

Fig. 1   Structure of a typical agaric.

The volva or sheath

When the mushroom grows and the universal veil breaks its remains surround the base of the stem, forming the volva or sheath. If the very bottom of the fruit-body is examined carefully, a cup-shaped socket may often be found. This is sometimes indicated only by a swollen ridge around the base of the stem or by a few rows of scales.

The cap

The shape of the cap is a point of prime importance in the determination of species. It can be almost flat, it may be convex, or it may have a central boss. Sometimes it may be convex above and flat below; in many species there can be a central depression. A few species are funnel-shaped, such as the chanterelle. The texture of the cap may be scaly, or silky and smooth; in some species it is viscous or slimy.

The gills

The gills, which are the spore-bearing part of the plant, look rather like flat plates crowded together under the cap, radiating from the centre. The manner in which they are attached to the stem is a very important diagnostic characteristic. Fig. 2 shows the various ways in which they can be attached. If they are not joined to the stem at all they are called 'free'; if they just barely touch the stem they are said to be 'adnexed'. If the gills are attached to the stem along their whole width they are called 'adnate', but if they curve inwards towards the stem so that their attachment is somewhat hooked, they are known as 'sinuate'. In some species the gills run down the stem for some distance; these are called 'decurrent'. The gills are also said to be 'distant' when they are widely spaced apart, and 'crowded' when they are close together.

The spores

The colour of the spores is, as we have seen, a characteristic feature, but only in mature specimens; young specimens have colourless spores. In mature specimens, if the colour cannot be easily detected, it is a simple matter to make a spore print. This shows not only the colour of the spores, but also the pattern of the gills, indicating whether they are distant or crowded.

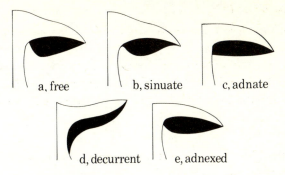

a, free   b, sinuate   c, adnate

d, decurrent   e, adnexed

Fig. 2 Arrangement of gills in agarics.

How to make a spore print To obtain a spore print cut off the stalk and lay the cap face (gills) downwards on a sheet of white paper if the gills are dark, or black paper if they are white or pale pink. Cover with an inverted tumbler or jam-jar in order to prevent air currents or draughts causing any movement, and leave undisturbed for about twelve hours – overnight is ideal.

Remove the glass and lift the cap of the mushroom very carefully, without dragging any part of it across the surface of the paper, which would smudge the spore print. The imprint of the gills, showing their arrangement and the spore colour, will be found on the paper. The spores may be white, pink, rose-coloured, yellow, brown, rust-coloured, purplish or black; all these colours denote various sub-groups and are a great help in the identification of the mushroom.

Fig. 3 shows another method of making a spore print, in which the stem is not removed but passed through a hole just big enough to admit it in a sheet of stiff card, which is then placed across the top of a tumbler or jam-jar. If you use this method you must place the jar in such a spot that no movement of air can dislodge the cap while the print is being formed.

Mycologists (botanists who study fungi) frequently make spore prints of all the various species they have collected on a 'fungus foray', as such collecting trips are called. They then preserve them by spraying them with a colourless matt varnish, which has the effect of gumming the spores in position so that they will not be dislodged. The cards are then covered with a sheet of clingfilm or plastic for protection, and filed in systematic order.

Fig. 3   Making a spore print.

The stem

The stem can either be cylindrical or fusiform (spindle-shaped). It may be rigid or flexible, it may have a shiny, polished appearance, or it may be rough or fibrous. It may be hollow, solid or filled with a loose cotton-like substance. The colour and texture are important features.

Finally

So, if we are to be certain of our identification and be quite sure that the mushrooms we put into the pot will not make us very ill or even kill us, it behoves us to know and learn the various features. Remember that the main things to look for are: the colour of the spores, the method of attachment of the gills, the presence or absence of a volva and/or a ring, the texture and colour of the stem, the shape, texture and colour of the cap, and whether any milky juice exudes from the flesh when cut or whether it changes colour. All these points will be elaborated in the descriptions of the individual species.

The ones to avoid

Nowhere in the field of wildfood gathering is correct identification more vital than when mushroom hunting. In Britain we have four deadly species (shown in Fig. 4) which are usually fatal, and another dozen or so which, although not lethal, would make you so ill that the painful and unpleasant symptoms could well put you off mushroom hunting for good. That would be a great pity, since you would be depriving yourself of enjoying the ones which are such good eating; some are so delicious that they are a gourmet's delight, and you will wonder why you did not try them sooner! But first I must describe the ones to avoid.

DEATH CAP *(Amanita phalloides)*

This is the deadliest of Britain's four most highly toxic fungi. Its name is well-deserved, since it is responsible for perhaps 90% of all the fatalities caused by mushroom poisoning. It is in fact the most dangerous fungus known, and the consumption of only a minute quantity will cause intensely painful symptoms, usually followed by a lingering and agonising death. Superficial resemblances between this species and certain edible mushrooms have doubtless been responsible for these tragedies. However, there are sufficient differences, as opposed to similarities, which can be learned and committed to memory. This is the only safeguard.

1. The gills of the death cap are always white at all stages of growth, and never darken or change colour with age.
2. The gills are free from the stem (see Fig. 2).
3. The stem has a ring, easily visible in young specimens, less apparent in more mature ones but still discernible.
4. The base of the stem is sheathed in a cup-like volva (see Fig. 1) which is usually buried in the soil, though sometimes, in light, friable soils, the loose irregular upper edges may show above the

Fig. 4 The deadly four: (a) Death cap, (b) Destroying angel, (c) Red-staining inocybe, (d) Leaden entoloma.
- Gills *white* in all four, but becoming pinkish in (d) with age.
- Ring round stem in (a) and (b); no ring in (c) or (d).
- Volva (bulbous sheath) at base in (a) and (b); no volva in (c) or (d).

surface. The mushroom hunter must therefore dig out white mushrooms and unequivocally reject any of them which have this characteristic volva at the base. It is a diagnostic feature of *A. phalloides*.

The cap is at first egg-shaped; as it expands it becomes convex or flattened. It can measure from 2 to 4 inches (5-10cm) in diameter. Its colour is typically light olive or yellowish, with a few darkish streaks, especially near the centre.

A variety sometimes occurs in which the cap is pure white, but it is rather uncommon. This has been given specific status by some botanical authorities as *Amanita verna*, while others consider it to be merely an albino form of *A. phalloides*. Whatever its botanical status, it still has all the other distinctive features of *A. phalloides*, and is not one whit less deadly.

In young specimens there may remain on top of the cap a few torn fragments of the white membrane or 'veil' that covers the fungus as it emerges above the surface of the earth, but these soon disappear. The cap is smooth when dry, but slightly slimy when moist.

The stem is white, occasionally with a slight pale yellowish or greenish tinge, and is smooth, with a few closely-adhering scales just below the ring. It is rather slender, narrower at the top and usually longer than the diameter of the cap. The stem becomes hollow in old specimens. The ring is attached to its upper part, white above and pale yellowish below, thin, and hanging downwards like a frill. It is easily rubbed off, but one can usually see where it was attached.

The gills are white, crowded and free from the stem, and the ends adjacent to the stem are rounded. The spores are white. The flesh is soft and white, and the cap peels easily. The fungus has a sweetish smell, more pronounced in older specimens.

The death cap is common in deciduous woodlands and is sometimes found in adjoining grasslands. It is mainly a summer species, sometimes continuing to appear until mid-autumn, especially in warm seasons.

Learn to identify this most deadly mushroom, which causes many fatal cases of poisoning every year, especially on the Continent, where wild mushroom gathering for the pot is more commonly practised than in Britain (though I am, of course, hoping to change all that!). Once you have compared a specimen with any edible white agaric of equivalent size, you will never again confuse them.

DESTROYING ANGEL *(Amanita virosa)*

No less poisonous than the death cap is this closely related species, but far fewer deaths have been attributed to it, purely and simply because it is quite rare. It grows, where it occurs, in both deciduous and coniferous woodlands in summer and autumn. It should be noted that this species does not grow in open grassland. Pure white throughout, it does not attain the size of *A. phalloides*.

The cap, which is slightly viscid, is at first distinctly conical, often asymmetrical, giving it what John Ramsbottom, the eminent authority on fungi, has succinctly described as 'rather a tipsy look'. The central boss is always retained, even when the cap is fully expanded.

The white stem, which rises from a membranous volva, is slender and covered with woolly-looking scales, and frequently grows curved rather than straight. The silky white ring is usually lower on one side, remaining attached to the edge of the cap at several points. The gills are pure white with rounded, flaky-looking edges, and the flesh is white, with white spores. The fungus has a heavy, cloying smell.

Fatal cases of poisoning have been caused by collectors confusing this species with St. George's mushroom (*Tricholoma gambosum*), the horse mushroom (*Psalliota arvensis*) and other white-capped agarics. Remember that no edible agaric has white gills; they may be pale pink or some shades of beige, but *never* white. Nor do edible species ever have any cup-like structure at the base of the stem. You are unlikely to make any fatal errors of identification if you remember these two basic rules.

Avoid gathering any wild mushroom in the undeveloped 'egg' or 'button' stage, as the gills cannot be seen until the cap begins to expand and the enveloping veil is torn. There are cases on record where people have been poisoned by gathering the early stages of white-capped poisonous species which looked exactly like the young specimens of their edible counterparts. So – if not grown, leave alone!

RED-STAINING INOCYBE *(Inocybe patouillardii)*

The common and scientific names of this mushroom are certainly a mouthful, but just be sure you never take a mouthful of this species, as it could be your last.

The red-staining inocybe – one of Britain's four really dangerous species – has been eaten, both in Britain and on the Continent, with fatal results, but it is difficult to imagine what edible species it could have been confused with. Although entirely pure white and silky at first, if touched in any way, even superficially without breaking the skin, it immediately becomes stained with blotches of bright sealing-wax red, a characteristic which at once serves to distinguish it from any edible species, none of which ever develops discoloured streaks or blotches if handled. This mushroom also acquires the bright red staining naturally with age, on both cap and stem.

The red-staining inocybe is not normally a very common species, but in some years it appears much more abundantly than usual in its grassy habitats in the southern counties, especially after a season of heavy rains. Unlike many other fungi, it is a late spring and summer species, occurring in parkland and deciduous woodlands, where it is usually found in clearings, beside paths, at the edges of woods adjoining open land, and in similar light and open situations.

The cap is fleshy, from 1 to 3 inches ($2^1/2$-$7^1/2$cm) in diameter, conical at first, then flattened with a prominent central boss. The edges of the cap are frequently folded or lobed, even in young specimens, giving it a very irregular shape, and as the cap expands with growth, it may split from the edge inwards.

The stem is fibrous, without any ring, fairly stout, firm and solid, and usually narrower at the top, where its surface appears somewhat mealy. The gills are crowded, narrow and almost free from the stem; at first white, they later become olive-brown with white edges. The spores are the exact shade which artists call raw sienna. The fungus has a pleasant fruity smell, which may in some cases have been a misleading factor to the unfortunate persons ignorant of its identity.

When gathering any white mushroom, press the cap or stem with a fingernail, or cut the edge; if no red stain appears it is not *Inocybe patouillardii*, but check against the descriptions of other white mushrooms in case it may be another poisonous species. Remember – if in doubt, go without!

LEADEN ENTOLOMA *(Entoloma lividum)*

This is a highly toxic mushroom which causes a number of serious cases of poisoning, some fatal, every year. Unlike the death cap and the destroying angel, where the symptoms do not appear until twelve to twenty-four hours after eating, the symptoms of poisoning by the leaden entoloma are rapid in their onset, appearing from twenty minutes to two hours after its consumption. Violent retching and vomiting, accompanied by equally violent purging, are the main symptoms, which may take a week or more to subside; in several cases death has resulted. The leaden entoloma is frequently mistaken for St. George's mushroom (*Tricholoma gambosum*), which it resembles particularly when young. Don't make the same mistake or it may be St. Peter rather than St. George you'll be meeting rather sooner than you had expected.

The gills of the leaden entoloma, though white at first, soon become flesh-pink as the spores develop; it is this characteristic more than any other which has led to confusion with the pink-gilled *T. gambosum*. Furthermore, the leaden entoloma has a pleasant smell and taste which has lulled many an unwary experimenter into a false sense of security, so that by eating more than originally intended the symptoms were intensified. The cap is also firm and fleshy, like that of St. George's mushroom. However, the leaden entoloma appears much later, usually in summer and autumn, and seldom, if ever, before the end of May, whereas St. George's mushroom is a spring species, being found mainly from late April (23 April is St. George's Day, hence the name) into May. The leaden entoloma grows in open deciduous woods, sometimes in numbers, but is not found everywhere; it is locally very common in parts of the Midlands.

The cap, which can reach a diameter of 5 inches (12½cm), has a shiny, silky look, but is never viscid. It is convex at first, later becoming wavy-edged and irregular. It is smooth and of a greyish-beige or greyish-ochre colour, and the central boss is not very pronounced. The skin cannot be peeled off easily.

The stem is whitish, finely striated, rather short and stout, firm and solid, and often slightly club-shaped at the base. There is no ring or volva. It frequently grows more curved than straight.

The gills, which are white only in the very young stage, soon assume a salmon-pink colouration as the spores, which are a dull pink, mature. Occasionally they exhibit a yellowish tinge at their edges. They are somewhat crowded and, though at first touching the stem, later become almost free. The flesh is white, thick and firm-textured, and has a distinct mealy smell.

Avoid the leaden entoloma, despite its attractive appearance, pleasant smell and firm 'mushroomy' texture. You could, at the very least, end up in hospital at the wrong end of a stomach pump.

The four species just described are the four most deadly mushrooms in Britain or, indeed, in Europe where they also occur, but there are several others which must also be avoided. These, although not normally fatal, can cause most unpleasant and painful symptoms including vomiting, stomach pains, intestinal cramps, diarrhoea, hallucinations and disturbed vision. I will now describe these species. One or two of them do not have popular English names.

FLY AGARIC *(Amanita muscaria)*

This is the very common and conspicuous 'gnomes' toadstool', bright red with irregular white blotches (the remains of the ruptured veil), which makes such an attractive picture on those greeting cards showing autumn woodland scenes. It is distinctive enough to need no further description. You will note that the gnomes are always shown sitting on it, but never eating it, for it is highly toxic! The fly agaric is shown in Fig. 5.

PANTHER CAP *(Amanita pantherina)*

This is another member of the poisonous *Amanita* genus to avoid. It is sometimes known as the 'false blusher'. It can be found fairly commonly in deciduous woods from August to October. The cap is about 4 inches (10cm) in diameter and is brownish, dotted with white irregular blotches just like *A. muscaria*, and the edge of the cap is frequently finely-striated. The crowded gills are white and free from the stem, which is about 4 inches (10cm) high, swollen at the base where it emerges from the volva, and white with a shining, silky appearance with a thin, irregular ring. The flesh and the spores are white.

Both the white blotches on the cap and the ring are easily washed off by rain, or disintegrate with age, and the mushroom can then be confused with similar-looking ringless agarics with a smooth, brownish cap. The panther cap, however, has a strong smell of raw potatoes, which will help to distinguish it. The diagnostic feature of the volva is typical of *Amanita* species and is not found in edible agarics. The panther cap is shown in fig. 5.

Fig. 5 **Avoid, avoid!** (a) Fly agaric, (b) Panther cap, (c) False death cap, (d) Yellow-staining mushroom, (e) Sickener, (f) Verdigris agaric, (g) Crested lepiota, (h) Sulphur-tuft.

- Gills *white* in (a), (b), (c), (d) (darkening with age), (e), (g); *purple* in (f); *yellowish-green* in (h).
- Ring present in (a), (b), (c), (d), (e), (g); no ring in (f) and (h).
- Volva present in (a), (b), (c); no volva in (d), (e), (f), (g), (h).

FALSE DEATH CAP *(Amanita citrina)*

This is the *A. mappa* of the older books, but *citrina* is a more descriptive specific name, referring to the lemon-yellow colour of the cap. This, however, often appears more whitish, owing to the presence of remnants of the veil adhering in patches. The crowded white gills are free from the stem.

The stem is about 4 inches (10cm) tall, white, and striated above the ring, and is grossly swollen at the base, almost like an onion shape. The spores are white. The ring is white, striated above, downy beneath and drooping. The flesh is white and this species too has a smell of raw potatoes, though less pronounced than that of the preceding species. The false death cap (Fig. 5) grows in pine and beech woods and is quite common from August to October.

YELLOW-STAINING MUSHROOM
(Psalliota xanthoderma)

The white cap of this species stains bright yellow when bruised, so this species can be easily eliminated by pressing the cap with your thumbnail. The cap is about 3 inches (7½cm) across, smooth, and easily separates from the stem, frequently falling off as it is picked. The crowded, free gills are white to start with, then turning pink and finally brownish with the increasing age of the mushroom. The spores are a purplish chocolate-brown.

The stem, which reaches about 3 inches (7½cm) in height and is white, tinged yellowish at the base, also stains bright yellow if bruised. The ring is thin, white and membranous, the flesh white. The mushroom has a rather unpleasant smell, rather like carbolic soap. It is a fairly common species of parks and pastureland, appearing from August to October. This mushroom is shown in Fig. 5.

SICKENER *(Russula emetica)*

Both the popular and the scientific name of this one are descriptive enough, so all you have to do is to give it a wide berth. It's easily spotted, being a bright red (though the shade of red is different from that of the fly agaric – it's a more 'rosy' red), and although most books give the diameter of the cap as 3 inches (7½cm), I have found them considerably bigger. One I found was a good 5 inches (12½cm), though this is, perhaps, unusual. It is shiny and slimy-looking, and the colour fades in older specimens to a sort of muddy pink. The skin peels easily. It is shown in Fig. 5.

The gills are white and free from the stem, and the spores are white. The stem is about 3 inches (7½cm) high, solid and rather brittle, and pure white without any ring. This mushroom is very common in woods and wooded scrub from August to November.

VERDIGRIS AGARIC *(Stropharia aeruginosa)*

This is a very pretty verdigris-green species, easily recognisable. It is usually very small, seldom more than 2 inches (5cm) across the cap, which is slimy. The gills are adnate (see Fig. 2) and violet at first, becoming dark brown with maturity. The spores are purple. The stem grows up to 3 inches (7½cm) tall, and is whitish-green and slimy, with a whitish ring. The mushroom smells strongly of radishes. The flesh is pale green. The species is not particularly common but grows in beechwoods from July to November, and occasionally in pinewoods. This species is shown in Fig. 5.

CRESTED LEPIOTA *(Lepiota cristata)*

This is a strong and unpleasant-smelling relative of the edible and delicious parasol mushroom (*L. procera*). Unlike the latter species, the crested lepiota does not grow to any great size, 1½ inches (3½cm) in diameter being about average. The white cap has a reddish-brown central disc of granulose scales. The white gills are free and crowded, and very thin. The stem is pinkish-white and very fragile, growing to about 5 inches (12½cm) in height; it is slender, smooth and silky, and usually reddish-brown at the base. The ring is white, thin and membranous, rather inconspicuous, and frequently disappears altogether with age. (See Fig. 5).

The flesh is pinkish-white. The mushroom grows in parks, gardens and pastureland, frequently on lawns and compost heaps. It is fairly common and occurs from August to November.

SULPHUR-TUFT *(Hypholoma fasciculare)*

This, as its name implies, grows in tufts (the specific name *fasciculare* means 'in bundles') mainly on beech trees, appearing at any time from April to October, and is exceedingly common. It should not be confused with the edible honeytuft *(Armillaria mellea)* which will grow on the trunk of practically any tree and is, if anything, even more common, but which appears much later in the year, rarely before September. The cap of the sulphur-tuft is about 2 inches (5cm) across, sulphur-yellow with adnate gills (see Fig. 2) which are crowded and yellowish-green, darkening with age. The spores are purple, the flesh is yellow. The stem is about 4 inches (10cm) tall, hollow, yellow and often curved. There is no distinct ring, but occasionally a faint scar can be seen. The fungus has an unpleasant odour. (Fig. 5).

BOLETUS LURIDUS

The boletus mushrooms belong to an entirely different group from the agarics. The cap is spongy rather than fleshy, and instead of in gills the spores are contained in a network of tiny tubes, the open ends of which are called the pores. The stems are thick and stockily-built, never slender, and usually bulging out at the base. They have no ring or volva, which are strictly agaric features. The skin of the cap is usually a different colour from the underside, though not invariably.

The genus contains a number of very good edible species such as the cep *(Boletus edulis)*, which plays such an important part in French and German cookery. The one now to be described, however, is highly-toxic. Fortunately it is easy to recognise; its specific name *luridus* gives some indication of its appearance. It is the stem which is a garish mixture of brilliant purple and yellowish-ochre, not the cap, which is a plain beige colour. The hues of the stem are combined in a coarse network of veins, not unlike the lurid pictures in some medical books showing the veins of the human body. Combined with this off-putting appearance, the fungus has a sour smell. The pores (the underside of the cap) are rust-red.

B. luridus is found in beech and oak woods, especially on chalk soils. It is also partial to parkland where lime trees grow. It may be found from June to September. The cap can be up to 6 inches (15cm) across, but is usually rather smaller.

BOLETUS SATANUS

In an attempt to translate the specific name of this fungus into 'popular' English, some writers have called it the 'devil's boletus'. It can cause very violent symptoms of enteric poisoning, so the name is apt.

This is another large species; a 6 inch (15cm) cap is quite common. The stem has a coarse network of veins, as in the preceding species, but these are darker in colour, lighter beneath the cap. The cap itself is a pale whitish-green; the pores are bright red. This fungus does not have much odour. The flesh is white, becoming blue when broken. This species is confined mainly to southern England and grows on chalk soils only.

BOLETUS PIPERATUS

This boletus is not 'poisonous' in the usually-understood sense of the word, but its taste is unacceptably pungent, hot and peppery – a tiny portion touched to the tip of the tongue tastes like a mouthful of raw chillies! The species is easily recognised as it has a much more slender stem than most other species of this genus, rust-coloured spores, a cinnamon-coloured cap and a chrome-yellow patch at the base of the stem. It is in fact unusual in this group to have a species with 'matching' cap and stem.

The cap is shiny when dry and is much smaller than the other two boletus species just described, seldom more than 3 inches (7½cm) and usually smaller. It has very little scent. This little boletus is widely distributed and is found in both deciduous and coniferous woods.

The three poisonous boletus species are shown in Fig. 6.

Fig. 6 (a) Boletus luridus; (b) Boletus satanus; (c) Boletus piperatus. All are poisonous.

The edible mushrooms

We come now to the edible mushrooms – after all, these are the ones which this book is all about! As already mentioned, in Britain alone we have at least a hundred edible species. Some are perhaps more edible than others; a few, while perfectly edible and innocuous, may be insipid to the taste, or their texture may tend to be leathery or woody and so they are not very good eating. You might break your teeth on them, but at least they would not poison you. Some of the recipes which I give later in the book recommend a particular species, but in a good many cases you may substitute others as and when available if they are a basically similar type of mushroom.

Some general guidelines when collecting fungi for food

1. Be certain that you know the species without any doubt. This is the first and unbreakable rule. Beginners should confine them-selves to the easily recognisable species, avoiding others until they are more experienced. Avoid any kind which has a cup-shaped socket at the bottom of the stem; to make sure of this you must dig up the mushroom and not merely pull it up or cut it off at the base. Avoid any fungi which have white gills or you may not live long enough to regret it.
2. Ignore any statements about 'easy ways of telling edible from poisonous kinds' or 'methods of preparation which destroy the poisonous properties'. These are all old wives' tales and have no foundation in fact whatsoever. They include such notions as a mushroom which changes colour in your hand after picking, or turns black if rubbed with a silver coin, and so on. All absolute rubbish! It would be interesting to know what percentage of fungus poisoning fatalities was caused by people believing such myths.
3. Gather only fairly young but well-grown specimens which are free from signs of decay and show no traces of attack by maggots.

Do not gather fungi immediately after heavy rain, when they are waterlogged and soft to the touch, since they then decompose far more rapidly owing to the abnormally high water content. Do not collect old specimens, since these will in all probability be riddled with the burrows of insects or their larvae. The mushrooms should be dry when collected.

4. Do not bruise collected mushrooms while carrying them home, because any bruised spots decompose very quickly. The best method is to place each specimen in a separate plastic bag and put all the bags carefully into a shallow basket. Do not tie the bags; air should be allowed to circulate, as this will help to prevent decomposition.

5. Do not wash fungi unless they are to be cooked immediately.

6. Do not keep fragile fungi for longer than one day. They must be kept in a cool place, spread apart so that they do not touch each other, and where air can circulate freely. Do not put in the refrigerator. The sturdier species may be kept for a day or two longer.

7. Do not re-heat leftover mushroom dishes.

8. If fungi have to be boiled in the process of cooking, pour off the water afterwards and do not use it for any other purpose.

9. Do not eat any mushroom uncooked. Very few fungi can be eaten raw.

Whichever kinds you use, one thing you *must* do is check them before use with a good illustrated botanical guide giving the identification of the species in the form of colour plates (photographs are usually a more accurate guide than coloured drawings). Some good reliable books for identification are listed at the end of this book. You can either take a pocket-sized book with you when going out on a fungus foray or, if the book you use is a large and heavy one, check your mushrooms when you return home and before you start cooking! If you find you have inadvertently gathered a harmful species, be sure to wash your hands thoroughly after destroying it, before starting to cook with the ones that are good.

Now for the ones to look for.

BLEWIT *(Tricholoma personatum)*
and WOOD BLEWIT *(T. nudum)*

These two are, to my mind, just about the most delicious of all our native wild mushrooms. They also share with some of the other good edible kinds a most welcome feature: owing to their distinctive colouration it is very unlikely that they could be confused with any other species.

A hundred years ago – but, regrettably, no longer – blewits were sold in London's Covent Garden market. Nowadays 'bluelegs', as they are called in the Midlands, are still occasionally sold on market stalls in that region, though far less frequently than used to be the case. I have seen them offered for sale in greengrocers' shops in Northampton, Rugeley, Cannock, Poynton and Crewe, but only sporadically in the last fifteen years. However, since they are quite common and fairly well-distributed, you should be able to find them without too much difficulty, from early October onwards, on pastures and downlands, often growing in large rings. The wood blewit, as its name implies, is more often associated with woodland; the edges of pinewoods seem to be its favoured habitat.

The cap of *T. personatum* is smooth, rounded and fleshy, from 2½ to 5 inches (6½-12½cm) in diameter, its edge characteristically overhanging the gills. With growth the cap tends to flatten out somewhat but, unlike the wood blewit, it never loses its original rounded look – a feature which helps to distinguish the two species. The colour of the cap is a pale beige.

The stem is very stout, short (usually not more than 3 inches, 7½ cm, high), solid and cylindrical, often swollen at the base. There is no ring. Its characteristic blue colouration is the diagnostic feature which will enable you to identify this very tasty mushroom without fear of confusion (except, possibly, with the next species, the wood blewit, which tastes just as good!). No other mushrooms have blue stems.

The gills are whitish at first but soon darken with increasing growth. They are broad and crowded and can easily be separated from the cap. The spores are pale pink. The flesh is white when dry, greyish when moist, and has a very pleasant odour.

The wood blewit (*T. nudum*) appears later than the preceding species, seldom being found before mid-October and continuing into late November. I have often found it even when there had been a sharp frost. It can frequently be found growing on old compost heaps, especially those which have dead leaves as their main constituent.

In colour it is much like the preceding species, but the blue tint is more of a delicate lilac and also tinges the cap, which usually grows larger than that of *T. personatum*; the cap of *T. nudum* can reach 5 or 6 inches (12½-15cm). I once found a beautiful 7-inch (18cm) specimen on Wimbledon Common; it weighed a pound and made a meal for four! Its shape is different from that of the previous species; at first convex, it soon becomes flattened, or even concave. Its margin is incurved and wavy. The colour of the cap darkens with age, as in *T. personatum*, but it never loses the characteristic lilac tinge.

The ringless stem is rather more slender than in *T. personatum* and the gills narrower, giving a more crowded appearance. As the cap expands with growth, the gills sometimes run down the stem slightly. They are bluish, never developing any brownish colouration; this is another point which will help you to distinguish between those two closely related species. Yet another diagnostic feature of the wood blewit is that the flesh, too, is bluish, unlike that of its relative. The spores are pinkish. The odour is less pronounced than that of *T. personatum* and can best be described as a faint but pleasant 'mushroomy' smell.

These two *Tricholomas* are shown in Fig. 7.

ST GEORGE'S MUSHROOM *(Tricholoma gambosum)*

Here we have another tasty Tricholoma species, but take good note of the distinguishing characteristics of this species, in order to avoid confusing it with the leaden entoloma, described on page 13, with which it can be, and unfortunately has been, confused. St. George's mushroom is found from the latter part of April until June (St. George's Day is 23 April, hence its name) and it is very partial to calcareous soils, though it also occurs in other habitats.

The cap looks very rounded, is up to 3 inches (7½cm) across, and is a pale creamy-white inclining to light yellowish in the centre, especially when moist. The skin is soft to the touch, like a kid glove. The stem is thick, short and cream-coloured, often curved or irregu-

Fig. 7   (a) Blewit (*Tricholoma personatum*); (b) Wood blewit (*T. nudum*); (c) St. George's mushroom (*T. gambosum*).
- (a), (c) cap rounded; (b) cap flattened.
- (a), (c) stem thick; (b) stem more slender.
- Gills in (a) separate from stem; (b) decurrent; (c) sinuate. (See Fig. 2).

lar in shape and slightly larger at the base. The gills are sinuate (see Fig. 2) and are whitish or pale cream, narrow and crowded. The spores are white. The flesh is solid, firm and white and may be up to 1 inch (2¹/₂cm) thick in the middle of the cap. When cut it gives off a strong odour of meal.

This mushroom grows in pastures or on open downland and its stocky appearance is reminiscent of blewits to which, of course, it is closely related.

St. George's mushroom is depicted in Fig. 7.

PARASOL MUSHROOM *(Lepiota procera)*

Specimens have been found measuring a foot (30cm) across. I have never found one that size, but in 1988 found one of 9 inches (22¹/₂cm) growing in Thetford Forest, and I have frequently gathered 7-inch (18cm) specimens and occasionally 8-inch (20cm) examples. Thus, to make a meal for four, you do not need more than one or two, as they are quite heavy when they reach that size. The species also grows

Fig. 8   Parasol mushroom (*Lepiota procera*).

quite tall, anything from 10 inches (25cm) to 14 inches (35cm) being quite usual. The mushroom is also very distinctive in appearance, as can be seen from Fig. 8. The only other species with which it can possibly be confused is the much rarer and much smaller *Lepiota rhacodes*, or shaggy parasol mushroom, which is also edible but less tasty, and, possibly, the poisonous crested lepiota (*L. cristata*) described on page 18. However, this latter species never grows to any great size and has a strong unpleasant smell. All in all, it's unlikely that you will confuse the good and tasty *L. procera* with any others in the genus.

It is quite common throughout Britain, occurring in both deciduous and coniferous woodland, especially on the edges of clearings and on the outskirts of copses, and sometimes on pastureland. I once found it growing abundantly on the golf course at Hayling Island. Where you find one you find several – it is very gregarious.

The cap has a typical pointed boss in the centre, is brownish in colour, and the rest of the cap is covered with brownish scales, giving it a rather roof-like or 'shingled' appearance. The background colour of the skin of the cap is greyish or very pale whitish-beige. The stem is also scaly and somewhat similar in colouration, sometimes darker. There is a whitish ring, and the base of the stem is thicker than the upper portion. It is found from July to October. The mushroom has a very pleasant scent.

Lepiotas are not very moist-fleshed and so they are slow to decay, and therefore they can be dried for winter and spring use. Thread a piece of fine string or cotton through the centres of the caps (having removed the stems completely) and hang up in a warm place. Knot the string or cotton between each cap so that they do not touch, thus facilitating the circulation of air around them so as to avoid mould developing. Don't hang mushrooms for drying in any part of the kitchen where steam from kettles or cooking will dampen them.

HORSE MUSHROOM *(Psalliota arvensis)*

The horse mushroom is very closely related to the common field mushroom (*P. campestris*) but grows much larger; the cap can grow up to 8 inches (20cm) across quite commonly, sometimes even larger. My experience is that the larger the cap the tastier the meat! (This applies to the ordinary field mushroom too, including the cultivated kind.) The 'button' stage is best avoided, as these mushrooms at that stage look little different from certain poisonous agarics to the uninitiated, but when they expand they are very different indeed and much less liable to be confused.

The horse mushroom is essentially a field species, never occurring in woodland. It is particularly common in cultivated fields. Its cap is rounded and ball-like in the early stages, creamy-white in colour, hence its French name of *boule de neige* (snowball), and has a smooth texture like a kid glove. It grows from June to October. The gills are dark brown when mature, and the spores purplish-brown. The stem is thick and white, becoming more distended at the base. The flesh is firm and white and has a strong 'mushroomy' smell. The taste is stronger than that of the common field mushroom, and thus it is particularly suited to the making of mushroom ketchup.

The horse mushroom is shown in Fig. 9.

TAWNY GRISETTE *(Amanitopsis fulva)*

This fungus has a good taste but, since it is rather small, you need to gather quite a lot of them to make them worth while cooking. Against this, they are as common as mud – or perhaps I should say

Fig. 9 Horse mushroom (*Psalliota arvensis*).

common *in* mud, because damp, boggy woods are where you are most likely to find plenty of them. Deciduous woods where there is a lot of leafmould humus are the best places to look. They also grow in mixed woodland, and occasionally in coniferous woodland. They are found throughout Britain. Usually where there is one there will be a dozen, so if you have found a good habitat you will most likely find them to be locally very common and thus be able to gather enough for the pot without having to walk miles.

The tan-coloured cap is small – seldom more than 1½ inches (4cm) in diameter – and has a distinctive striated edge and a prominent boss in the centre, as can be clearly seen in Fig. 10. The cap is very thin and insubstantial-looking and is easily knocked off the stem. The stem is fairly tall, up to 4 inches (10cm) high, and rather slender, and is easily broken. Such fragile little fungi tend to 'cook down' quite a bit, and you will therefore need to gather about four times as many as you *think* you will need. However, the taste is very rewarding and quite distinctive, as it is very delicate and unlike most other mushrooms.

The gills are white and free from the stem. The spores are whitish. The flesh is white, and there is little if any odour. This mushroom grows in summer and autumn. The caps may be dried for winter and spring use, threaded on cotton. This fungus, however, being so small, is best cooked together with other larger species. Not for nothing to the Germans call it 'the Dwindling'.

Fig. 10 **Tawny grisette** (*Amanitopsis fulva*).

FAIRY RING CHAMPIGNON *(Marasmius oreades)*

This is another small fungus, but it is firmer and tougher than the preceding species. It is very common and you are likely to find it on your first fungus foray and probably all your subsequent ones too. It is most abundant, in summer or autumn, after a rainy spell. This species is known by its popular name owing to its habit of growing in rings, so often seen on lawns, parks and downlands. It is found throughout Britain.

The cap is smooth, 1 to 2 inches (2½-5cm) across, and can be rounded or flattened according to age, but it always has a rounded protuberance or boss in the middle. This is less conical than that of the preceding species; the present species also does not have the striated edge to the cap. Apart from these two main differences, the two species are not dissimilar in appearance. The colour of *M. oreades* is slightly darker if anything than that of *Amanitopsis fulva*; one book describes it as 'reddish buff'. The stem is about the same colour, very straight and slender. Unlike that of the preceding species, the stem does not snap easily when handled.

The gills are pale buff-coloured, thick, broad and set rather far apart. They are alternately long and short, the long ones not being

Fig. 11   Fairy ring champignon (*Marasmius oreades*).

fastened to the stem. This alternation of length in the gills is another diagnostic feature, but only on close examination. The flesh is whitish, and the odour very pleasant, especially when the fungus is dried. One author has likened its scent to that of clover. Drying is, in fact, the best way to use this fungus. It has the very useful quality from the culinary point of view of shrivelling to a small volume when dried and swelling up to full size and smoothness again when reconstituted with any kind of liquid, such as when added to soup. The stems are too tough to be used, and should be discarded.

Fig. 11 shows this mushroom.

GIANT PUFFBALL *(Lycoperdon giganteum)*

We go now from one extreme to the other – from tiny, delicate fungi to one the size of a football – or bigger!

The puffballs belong to a different group from the agarics (the gilled fungi we have been talking about so far) and make a welcome change. Usually only the largest member of this family, the giant puffball, is used in cookery. This is not because other members of the family are inedible, but because they are edible only in their early stages and, at that stage, can easily be confused with certain members of a related group which can cause serious gastric disturbances, even if they are not exactly deadly. It is therefore deemed prudent to stick to the distinctive *L. giganteum*. At least it is so big that it cannot possibly be confused with anything else.

The giant puffball (see Fig. 12) is quite common in summer and early autumn in meadows and the grassy parts of woods, even in gardens where the right conditions exist – grassed areas with plenty of compost and humus. The young specimens are spherical, but with approaching maturity the mushroom becomes more pumpkin-shaped, wider than it is high, or a flattened oval. The outer skin is creamy-white and as smooth as kid. At first the interior is also firm and white, with the consistency of a firm but soft white cheese. Only in this condition is the fungus fit for eating – and delectable it is, too. Later, as the spores ripen, the interior becomes a powdery mass, first yellowish and then a brownish-olive. The skin then bursts open in several places, emitting clouds of spores.

The giant puffball should therefore be sought early, up to about the end of August, since by September the spores will be fast developing. The skin should be peeled off and the flesh cut into strips about half an inch thick for frying; they can be coated with egg and breadcrumbs, like cutlets. Thicker slabs may also be coated with batter and fried in deep fat, while little specimens can be eaten whole cooked in this manner.

Dorothy Hartley, in her book *Food in England*, has quite a lot to say about the giant puffball. She says that the texture and flavour are exactly like sweetbreads, and that one can sometimes be a feast in itself. 'I remember', she says, 'a huge one found by a shepherd of the

Fig. 12   **Giant puffball** (*Lycoperdon giganteum*).

wolds near Loughborough. It was about 24 inches in diameter. We cut it in slices, egg-and-breadcrumbed them and fried them, and one giant puffball served six people'.

MOREL *(Morchella esculenta)*

This fungus, which is not very common, is widely distributed and sometimes locally frequent in a particular area. However, it does take a bit of finding. It occurs in spring in the clearings in woods, especially on calcareous soils, though it is not confined to these habitats. See Fig. 13.

The morel belongs to a group in which the spores are contained in little sacs, which give the fungus its characteristic 'honeycombed' appearance. The cap is usually dark brownish or blackish, but in some specimens can be lighter. The fungus is quite small, usually about 2 to 3 inches (5-7^1/$_2$cm) high, on a short and stocky white stem, which is grooved at the base. The cap itself is normally about 3 inches (7^1/$_2$cm) in width when mature. Its shape is rounded, sometimes more or less pointed at the apex. Both cap and stem are hollow.

Morels have been known and appreciated by gourmets for hundreds of years. They can be used both fresh and dried. Before cooking

Fig. 13 **Morel** *(Morchella esculenta).*

they should be carefully cleansed of any grit or other 'foreign bodies' (some with six legs!) that may be lurking in the pits.

CHANTERELLE *(Cantharellus cibarius)*
HORN OF PLENTY *(Craterellus cornucopioides)*

These two mushrooms, shown in Fig. 14, are closely related and can be cooked in exactly the same recipes.

The chanterelle is unmistakable from its colour alone – a brilliant yellow like the yolk of an egg. The species affects beech and oak woods, birch plantations and pinewoods alike; it is fairly catholic in habitat. It is frequently found beside well-trodden paths and roads through such wooded country. It occurs from July to November, but only after a damp season, when it can be quite common in its favoured localities.

The gills and the cap appear continuous, and the overall shape is funnel-like, with wavy edges and lobes. It has a pleasant apricot-like smell. It is about 2 to 3 inches (5-7$^{1}/_{2}$cm) across and about 3 inches (7$^{1}/_{2}$cm) high. The stem is the same bright yellow colour as the cap. Gills that run down the cap in this way are known as decurrent (see Fig. 2). Despite the overall yellow colour, the spores are white. The flesh is white, thick in the middle, becoming thinner towards the edges, sometimes also becoming yellowish near the margin.

Fig. 14   (a) **Chanterelle** (*Cantharellus cibarius*); (b) **Horn of plenty** (*Craterellus cornucopioides*).

The horn of plenty is almost exactly the same shape as the chanterelle, but its stem is usually longer. Its colour is brownish or bluish-black. It grows in both deciduous and coniferous woods. It is especially common in beechwoods and in hazel coppices, and it has a predilection for shady places where it is often hidden among leaves and undergrowth. If you look for it assiduously you usually manage to find it – at least I do. What makes it much more difficult to find than the chanterelle is its dark colour, which blends into the background; it is certainly not rarer than the chanterelle, rather the reverse.

In size the horn of plenty is about the same size as its relative, perhaps slightly taller and with a slightly narrower stem. It appears much later in the year, in August and September.

SAFFRON MILK CAP *(Lactarius deliciosus)*

The specific name *deliciosus* is a very apt description! I happened to be on a fungus foray not so long ago and found quite a large colony of them growing in our local woods. I cooked them for my lunch – they were lovely!

This mushroom looks rather like a Tricholoma with its stocky appearance, thick stem and low stature and, in some specimens, the shape of the cap; however, it is not closely related, and there are several differences. When the cap is cut, it exudes a saffron (reddish-orange) milky juice. The cap itself can be up to 4 or 5 inches (10-12½ cm) across, at first slightly convex with an inrolled margin, but later with maturity the central part reverses inwards into a fairly well-defined concavity. The colour is orange, or brick-coloured in some specimens, often a combination of the two, with concentric markings (not in clear rings but irregular) in the darker shade. Older specimens sometimes have greenish tinges which look like stains or blotches. These are not harmful when cooked, but younger specimens which do not show these green blotches are always preferable to the more mature examples.

The stem is more or less the same shade as the cap but paler. It stains verdigris-green when bruised (at any age). Soon after the mushroom has attained a reasonable size the stem, which averages about 2½ inches (6½cm) in height, becomes hollow. The gills, which are narrow and crowded and the same saffron colour as the other parts, are decurrent (see Fig. 2). The spores are pinkish, and the flesh is off-white, becoming orange when cut or broken, and green if the cut surface is exposed to the air for any length of time. The mushroom has a slight but pleasant 'fruity' odour. It is an early autumn species.

The saffron milk cap is not uncommon and occurs in coniferous woods, by roadsides near or passing through pinewoods, and on open land in the vicinity of pines.

If saffron milk caps have to be chopped prior to cooking, do this immediately before they go into the pot. You will thus avoid the green discolouration mentioned above. While not toxic in any way, it may be found off-putting by some.

The stem should not be used in cooking. When cooked it becomes rather hard and woody, so it is unlikely that you would eat it anyway.

This mushroom is depicted in Fig. 15.

SHAGGY INK CAP OR LAWYER'S WIG
(Coprinus comatus)
INK-CAP *(Coprinus atramentarius)*

WARNING: These two mushrooms are both excellent edible species, but *must not be consumed at the same time as alcohol*. Not only must you not drink wine, beer, cider or spirits with the meal, but you must not eat either of these mushrooms within twenty-four hours of having partaken of, or intending to partake of, any alcoholic substance. These mushrooms have been found to contain a substance identical to the active ingredient of the drug Antabuse which is used in the aversion therapy treatment of alcoholism. It causes violent vomiting and nausea. Commit this little couplet to memory:

Wigs and ink caps do not choose
If you want a glass of booze!

The shaggy ink cap or lawyer's wig is unmistakable. It looks for all the world like a huge white busby. It is a very common species and too large to escape notice even by the novice. It can, and often does,

Fig. 15   **Saffron milk cap** (*Lactarius deliciosus*).

grow up to 9 inches (22½cm) tall, and even young undeveloped specimens just coming up out of the earth are the size of a large hen's egg. The cylindrical white cap has a shaggy look owing to the loose scales with which it is covered. The top of the cap is usually covered with light brownish scales.

The shaggy ink cap grows very quickly – literally overnight – and in summer and autumn great quantities of them appear, especially after rain, in parks, gardens and commons and by the wayside, along the edges of woods and on agricultural land. It likes a lot of humus in the soil and is therefore particularly prevalent on compost heaps, manure heaps and rubbish dumps. Avoid taking specimens which may have been in contact with manure or sewage, rotting refuse and the like. You will find plenty of this common species growing in grass, where it is unlikely to be contaminated with harmful bacteria.

The gills are white at first, soon turning rose-pink and finally black. Gather the fungus only when the gills are white or pink. As soon as the gills have turned black, they dissolve into an inky black fluid (this process is called deliquescence) and the fungus is then useless as food. Young specimens, however, are very tasty, and Nilsson and Persson, in the second volume of *The Fungi of Northern Europe*, state that 'they can compete with any other mushrooms as delicacies for the table'.

The stem is white, silky in appearance, and at first bears a flimsy ring which is soon rubbed off and disappears. The stem is hollow, and the spores are black. The black inky fluid produced on deliquescence can be used for writing.

Fig. 16   (a) Shaggy ink cap or Lawyer's wig (*Coprinus comatus*). (b) Ink-cap (*C. atramentarius*).
- (a) cap shaggy; (b) cap smooth.
- (a) is much larger than (b).
- (a) grows separately; (b) grows in clusters.

The ink cap (*C. atramentarius*) is a close relative of the shaggy ink cap and is almost as common, but is considerably smaller. Its bell-shaped caps do not have a shaggy appearance as they do not have a scaly covering. Unlike the shaggy ink cap the smaller species grows in clusters. Their overall colour is greyish-white, with occasional touches of light brown, but this is not evident on all specimens. The stem is shorter in proportion to the cap than in *C. comatus*. The gills are light grey until they blacken and then become inedible although good to write with!

The 'Antabuse effect' of this species in combination with alcohol is even more severe than in the case of the shaggy ink cap. It is more slender and the stem has no ring. It appears at the same times of the year and affects lawns, old tree stumps and craters where old tree roots have not been completely dug out. Wooded parkland where felling has been taking place is a good habitat to look for it. This species also, of course, has black spores.

Both species are interchangeable as far as their culinary properties are concerned. Owing to their rapidly deliquescing tendency, these two species are particularly well-suited to making mushroom ketchup, but you must be very careful to remember to label the bottle with the name of the species and the warning that it must not be used at a meal in which wine is used in cooking one of the dishes or with which wine, beer, cider or spirits are served.

These two mushrooms are shown in Fig. 16, and the shaggy ink cap is also depicted in colour on the cover of this book.

EDIBLE BOLETUS *(Boletus edulis)*
ROUGH-STALKED BOLETUS *(B. scaber)*
ORANGE-CAPPED BOLETUS *(B. versipellis)*

These three mushrooms, shown in Fig. 17, will be taken together, since a recipe which will suit one boletus will usually suit another.

The edible boletus (*Boletus edulis*) is the famous *cèpe* of France, *Steinpilz* of Germany and 'penny bun mushroom' of the old English cookery books written in the days when a bun really did cost only a penny; whatever you have to pay for a bun these days, this boletus looks almost exactly like it, sitting atop a short stalk. It has a superb flavour and is eminently suitable for transforming a mediocre soup or an indifferent stew into an aromatic feast. It is one of the very best mushrooms for drying, and the commercially produced dried mushrooms imported from France and Germany and sold in up-market delicatessens here are usually this species.

You need not purchase supplies, however, as this boletus is a common denizen of both deciduous and coniferous woods, although I have found it most often in the latter. A warm and moist season will encourage the species to multiply profusely in its favoured habitats. From May to September the mushroom can be found, more commonly in the latter part of the season.

The boletus group of mushrooms do not have gills like the agarics, but they have a system of pores, giving the underside of the cap the appearance of a sponge. In the edible boletus this is whitish to pale yellowish, and when cut reveals white flesh. The cap, as we have seen, is bun-shaped and chestnut-brown – the exact shade of a well-baked bun. It can, however, grow up to 8 inches (20cm) across, in which case it looks more like a loaf!

The stem is very stout, basically cylindrical but frequently swollen and bulbous-looking. Towards the top it is covered with a fine

Fig. 17   (a) **Edible boletus** (*Boletus edulis*); (b) **Rough-stalked boletus** (*B. scaber*); (c) **Orange-capped boletus** (*B. versipellis*).

- (a) stem bulbous and swollen; (b) stem much more slender than (a); (c) stem thicker than (b) but much less so than (a).
- (a) and (c) have large caps; (b) has a much smaller cap.

network of raised white lines, tapering off and merging into the general whitish-fawn ground colour of the remainder of the stem. No boletus has a ring. The stems of boletus mushrooms can be used in cooking, if sound and undamaged by insects or mice. The tubular pores should be removed from the flesh before cooking; they can be detached very easily.

The rough-stalked boletus (*Boletus scaber*) has, as its name implies, a rough stem. It is a smaller species than *B. edulis* and appears in early autumn, principally in birch woods, though it can sometimes be found growing in pinewoods. The stem is much more slender than that of the edible boletus and it is usually striated with brownish, greyish or blackish interrupted lines, which are raised from the background surface, thus producing the 'rough' feel. The colour of the cap is a soft greyish-fawn or light brown. The shape is similar to that of the preceding species, and its surface has a 'moist' feel, absent in *B. edulis*. The flesh is white, and the pores also, becoming a dingy olive in old specimens. It is always best to choose firm, young specimens when gathering mushrooms of this group.

The orange-capped boletus (*B. versipellis*) can be distinguished, as its name implies, by its bright orange cap. It, too, has a rough stem, but it is thicker and more solid-looking than that of *B. scaber*. Crowded tufts of black scales on the stem, however, are responsible for the 'rough' characteristics of the stem in *B. versipellis*. This is another big species, growing up to 8 inches (20cm) tall and the same size across the cap. The pores are grey at first, fading to ochreous in time. The white flesh soon changes colour on cutting, but this does not affect the taste, which is excellent. The stem can be eaten if scraped first before cooking. The orange-capped boletus occurs between August and October and prefers birch-woods, usually growing actually under the trees, in some years profusely.

All in all, these three species are common enough to ensure that, if your fungus foray takes place during a month when all three occur, you are pretty sure to find at least one of them. I know of at least three woods in which birch grows as well as conifers, and in these woods all three species have turned up. A mixed coniferous and deciduous wood is one of the best places to hunt for fungi of any kind.

Boletus mushrooms are frequently called 'ceps', which is merely an anglicised version of the French *cèpe*, which, *sensu strictu*, refers to *Boletus edulis*, but for convenience the word 'ceps' will be used in the recipe section to mean any species of this group.

HONEYTUFT *(Armillaria mellea)*

You can hardly fail to find this species, shown in Fig. 18, since it is one of the commonest of all our woodland fungi. In one woodland glade you can find literally thousands of these mushrooms. The one thing you have to do is ensure that you can tell the difference between this species and the sulphur-tuft (*Hypholoma fasciculare*), which is described on page 19 and shown in Fig. 5.

The sulphur-tuft is bright yellow and has no ring; the honeytuft has a ring, and its colour is a brownish honey shade, with a darker brown central area. The honeytuft's cap is flatter-looking than the much more rounded cap of the sulphur-tuft. The present species is frequently spotted with darker brown, looking rather like freckles; the yellow species does not have these markings.

Fig. 18   **Honeytuft** (*Armillaria mellea*). **Compare it with the Sulphur-tuft (Fig. 5) which is inedible.**

The gills of the honeytuft are off-white in young specimens, becoming brownish with maturity, whereas the gills of the inedible species are greenish or yellowish and free from the stem; those of the honeytuft are decurrent (see Fig. 2). The colour of the spores, too, differs: in the honeytuft they are white, in the sulphur-tuft violet. Spore colour is one of the main bases for group division in fungi: *Melanosporae* (black-spored fungi), *Leucosporae* (white-spored fungi) and so on. The honeytuft is a late autumn species.

The stem can be from 4 to 6 inches (10-15cm) tall and is frequently curved, swelling very slightly towards the base. It is the same colour as the cap, paler above (sometimes whitish) and becoming darker towards the base. The flesh is white, off-white in older specimens. There is a barely discernible 'mushroomy' odour.

Since the honeytuft does not have a very strong or pronounced flavour, far less a distinctive one, it is most suitable pickled.

SPINDLE-SHANK *(Collybia fusipes)*
VELVET-SHANK *(C. velutipes)*

Fig. 19 shows these two very closely related agarics which have, like the honeytuft, a propensity for growing in clumps on old tree stumps

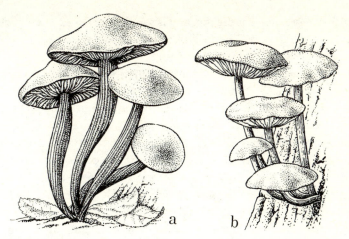

Fig. 19   (a) **Spindle-shank** (*Collybia fusipes*) (b) **Velvet-shank** (*C. velutipes*
- stem spindle-shaped in (a), not spindle-shaped in (b).
- cap larger in (a) than in (b).
- (a) gills fairly crowded; (b) gills distant (uncrowded).

and at the roots of living trees. From June until the autumn the spindle-shank can be found abundantly in deciduous woods, particularly in association with oak and beech trees, while the velvet-shank takes over where its relative leaves off, appearing in late autumn and carrying on through winter right up to spring. Indeed, this species is a very characteristic winter mushroom in a season when agarics are usually few and far between. Fortunately it is less particular than the spindle-shank about which trees to attach itself to, and can be found on most tree species of deciduous woods. If anything it is even commoner than the spindle-shank, which is a good thing too, as it is much the tastier of the two.

The spindle-shank's cap is between 1½ and 4 inches (4-10cm) in diameter, usually smaller rather than larger. It is rounded at first, soon assuming a somewhat flattened bell shape, ochraceous, reddish-brown or rust-coloured, often spotted with red or reddish, especially in older specimens. The gills are pale pinkish or whitish, becoming darker, even reddish, in mature specimens, often with red spots like the cap. The stem is a distinctive spindle shape, tapering almost to a point at the base; this feature should help to distinguish it from any other species of comparable size growing on a rotting log or tree stump. The stem has coarse longitudinal furrows and is reddish-brown, paler at the top, and is tough and firm, $2^1/2$ to 4 inches ($6^1/2$-10cm) in length. The flesh is whitish, with spores of the same colour, and has no discernible odour.

This mushroom is best used in conjunction with other species in soups, stews, etc., as its flavour is too mild to be particularly distinctive. The stem is too tough to be used. Young caps can be pickled in the same way as those of the honeytuft.

The velvet-shank is smaller, the cap being from $3/4$ to $2^1/2$ inches (2-$6^1/2$cm) in diameter. It is a smooth honey colour, darker in the centre, and slightly slimy when moist. It has a thin, transparent membrane at the edge through which the gills are discernible from above. These are distant (not set close together or crowded) and are a pale yellowish or beige with rounded lobe-like ends free from the stem. The stem is normally longer than the diameter of the cap, thus giving the mushroom a tall and slender appearance. It is quite thin, whitish just beneath the cap, and then deepening to yellowish on the way down and finally reddish, shading to chestnut-brown at the very bottom. The whole surface of the stem has a velvety look and texture; this is a diagnostic feature. The flesh is pale yellowish and has no discernible odour, and the spores are pale whitish.

This mushroom is described in Pilat and Ušák's *Handbook of Mushrooms* as 'a good edible mushroom which is suitable for soups and other dishes, and is highly valued as it grows when other mushrooms are not to be found'. I can hardly improve on this description, beyond saying that stews as well as soups can be improved by the addition of this species, either alone or with other kinds. I frequently use it in winter for omelets.

These very small and thin-capped species are not really the best choice for making into the more substantial dishes, such as those described in the recipes for large agarics, but they are ideal for adding taste to an otherwise bland dish, as a filling for pancakes, omelets and the like, or as an addition to bacon and eggs. They are also good added to a steak and kidney pie.

Part 2: RECIPES

Soups

A good many wild mushrooms are excellent for making soups if you have enough of them. For many of the recipes you can use quite a large selection of the various species, either together if you have several kinds, or if you have enough of one species you can just use that one. Here I give some general recipes for which you can use more or less any kind of mushrooms, and also some specific ones. In the case of a recipe for which only one particular species or group is suitable, I mention this at the beginning. Thus, if no particular species or group is recommended, you can use any kind you have available.

Cream of mushroom soup   *Serves 4*

225g/^{1}/$_2$lb mushrooms, sliced
1 small onion, peeled and sliced
275ml/^{1}/$_2$ pint white stock
25g/1oz butter

3 tablespoons single cream
3 level tablespoons plain flour
425ml/³/₄ pint milk
salt and pepper to taste
watercress to garnish

Cook the mushrooms and onion in the stock for about half an hour over a very low heat until soft. Allow to cool and rub through a sieve or run through the blender. In another pan melt the butter, stir in the flour to form a roux and cook for about 3 minutes. Remove from the heat and gradually stir in the milk; bring to the boil, immediately reduce the heat to its lowest setting, and stir continuously until the sauce thickens. Now add the mushroom purée and seasoning, stir well and simmer for 15 minutes. Remove from the heat and allow to cool slightly before stirring in the cream. To serve, re-heat without boiling (or it will curdle) and add a garnish of watercress.

Mushroom soup (1)   *Serves 3*

225g/¹/₂lb mushrooms
50g/2oz butter
275ml/¹/₂ pint milk
50g/2oz plain flour
1 tablespoon vinegar
bouquet garni
salt and pepper to taste
croûtons

Cover the mushrooms with cold water and add the vinegar. Bring slowly to the boil and simmer gently until the mushrooms are soft enough to be rubbed through a sieve, after cooling. Return the purée to the pan and keep hot. In another pan melt the butter, stir in the flour to make a roux, and gradually add the milk, stirring all the time. Season with salt and pepper and add the bouquet garni, tied in a muslin bag. Bring to the boil and boil for 3 minutes, then remove the muslin bag and add the mushroom purée. Stir well and serve hot with croûtons.

Mushroom soup (2)   *Serves 6-8*

350g/12oz mushrooms, minced
2 tablespoons flour
1 medium onion or leek
1.1 litre/2 pints vegetable stock
2 tablespoons fresh parsley, chopped
butter for cooking
salt and black pepper to taste

Heat the butter in a heavy frying pan, finely chop or mince the onion
or leek and cook until golden. Add the minced mushrooms and cook
until tender. Stir in the flour and the seasoning. When thoroughly
blended, pour into a large saucepan and add the stock, stirring
continuously over a medium heat until boiling point is reached.
Then reduce the heat and simmer for 30 minutes. Add the parsley
just before serving.

Mushroom soup (3)   *Serves 7-8*

450g/1lb mushrooms
2 tablespoons butter
2 tablespoons flour
1.1 litre/2 pints stock, any kind
2 egg yolks
275ml/¹/₂ pint single cream
salt and black pepper to taste

Mince the mushrooms, or chop very finely, and fry in the butter in a
heavy frying pan. Sprinkle in the flour, and when blended pour into a
saucepan. Add the stock and seasoning, bring to the boil, cover and
simmer for 30 minutes. Remove from the heat and put through a
sieve. Beat the egg yolks with the cream, add to the soup and re-heat,
stirring continuously. Make sure the soup does not boil, or you will
get scrambled eggs as well as curdled cream. Just heat through, no
more. Serve immediately.

Barley and mushroom soup   *Serves 6-8*

175g/6oz pearl barley
1.1 litre/2 pints vegetable stock

225g/¹/₂lb mushrooms
butter to cook
salt and white pepper to taste
pinch of nutmeg (optional)
2 tablespoons fresh parsley, chopped

Boil the barley in the stock until tender. Fry the mushrooms in some butter until cooked. When the barley is tender, add the mushrooms to the stock, season with salt and pepper and cook for a further 5 minutes over a very low heat. Serve sprinkled with parsley and a pinch of nutmeg, if liked.

Mushroom broth   *Serves 4*

This recipe is an Italian speciality and works best with ceps, or horse mushrooms with one or two ceps included. If you are using horse mushrooms but have no fresh ceps, it improves the flavour to add 15g/¹/₂oz dried ceps. For instructions for drying wild mushrooms, see page 111.

560g/1¹/₄lb fresh ceps *or* 560g/1¹/₄lb horse mushrooms and 15g/¹/₂oz
    dried ceps
3 tablespoons olive oil
2 cloves garlic, chopped
400g/14oz can peeled plum tomatoes
575ml/1 pint stock, any kind
50g/2oz Parmesan cheese, freshly grated
5 fresh basil leaves
salt and freshly-ground black pepper to taste
croûtons

If you are using horse mushrooms for this soup, soak the dried ceps in warm water for 15 minutes. Slice the fresh mushrooms. In a large pan fry the garlic in the oil for a short time, then add the sliced mushrooms and sauté for 10 minutes or so. At this point add the soaked dried ceps (if used) together with the liquid in which you have soaked them.

   Rub the tomatoes through a sieve and add them, with their juice, to the mushrooms in the pan. Cook over a medium heat for about 10 minutes, stirring frequently. Heat the stock in a separate pan, and when hot pour into the mushroom and tomato mixture. Season with salt and pepper, and when almost ready add the basil leaves. Serve with croûtons and sprinkle with grated Parmesan cheese.

Cep and bean soup   *Serves 4*

Ceps are the best kind of mushrooms to use for this soup. As to the beans, any kind will do – red kidney beans, haricot beans, black-eyed beans and so on. I use haricot beans myself – that is when I can find the ceps, which are rather thin on the ground in my area. The beans, whatever kind you use, must be soaked in water for 12 hours and then boiled for 2 hours before use.

175g/6oz fresh ceps
225g/8oz beans, cooked
3 tablespoons olive oil
1 large onion, peeled and sliced
1.1 litre/2 pints beef stock
salt and pepper to taste

Fry the onion in the olive oil in a large pan over a moderate heat for about 5 minutes. Slice the mushrooms and add to the pan, and continue cooking for a couple of minutes or so.

Pour off the water and put the beans into a saucepan with the stock and add the mushroom and onion mixture. Boil until thoroughly cooked, and season to taste. Serve with toasted slices of wholemeal bread.

Cream of cep soup   *Serves 4*

This really demands fresh ceps for the ultimate in flavour, but if you cannot find them use field mushrooms, adding 25g/1oz dried ceps, which can be purchased in some delicatessens. If the fresh ceps grow profusely in your area (I wish they did here!) choose the largest specimens, whose mature flavour is much better than that of the smaller young ones.

A good idea is to deep-freeze these delicious mushrooms if they grow plentifully in your area. They freeze very well indeed and, after thawing, can be sautéed just like fresh specimens.

450g/1lb fresh ceps *or*
    450g/1lb field mushrooms and 25g/1oz dried ceps

1 medium onion, peeled and minced
4 tablespoons olive oil
1.1 litre/2 pints beef stock
4 tablespoons single cream
salt and freshly-ground black pepper to taste
croûtons

Cut the fresh mushrooms into pieces. Cover the dried ceps with a little water and leave to soak. Fry the onion in the oil for 3 to 4 minutes, then add the mushrooms and sauté them for 6 to 7 minutes. In a separate pan bring the stock to the boil and simmer for 20 minutes; then add the mushroom and onion mixture, and finally add the ceps with the water in which you have soaked them. Stir well and simmer for about 30 minutes.

Remove the pan from the heat and allow to cool, then run the soup through the blender. Return it to the pan and add the cream and the seasoning. Stir continuously while reheating, taking care that it does not boil. Serve with croûtons.

The witch's brew   *Serves 4*

When you have returned from one of your fungus forays with rather fewer of any one kind than you had hoped, but quite a varied harvest representing a cross-section of the mushroom world, then this soup is probably the most appropriate one to make. It matters little which of the species you have collected, but you should have a good assortment.

225g/8oz assorted wild mushrooms
2 tablespoons butter
1 small onion, peeled and sliced
25g/1oz sweetcured bacon, cut into strips
1 small cooked potato, mashed
850ml/1½ pints beef or chicken stock
1 small carton single cream
2 tablespoons sour cream
2 egg yolks
2 tablespoons chives, finely chopped
salt and black pepper to taste

Cut the larger mushrooms into chunks but leave the small ones whole. Fry the onion in the butter in a large pan, and after a few minutes add the bacon and continue frying. Then add the mashed potato. Stir the mixture well and fry for a little longer.

Turn the mixture out into a saucepan, add the stock, stirring well, bring to the boil and simmer until everything is thoroughly cooked. Remove from the heat and stir in the cream, sour cream, beaten egg yolks, seasoning to taste and chives. Return to the heat for the shortest possible time, avoiding any risk of boiling. The soup is now ready to serve with slices of wholemeal bread and butter.

Mushroom and shallot cream soup   *Serves 4*

225g/8oz mushrooms, sliced
4 large shallots, finely sliced
50g/2oz butter
850ml/1$^{1}/_{2}$ pints stock, any kind
4 tablespoons single cream
salt and pepper to taste
chopped chives to garnish

Melt the butter in a frying pan and add the shallots. When these are soft but not browned, add the mushrooms, give the mixture a stir, and cover. Fry slowly until the mushrooms are cooked through. Bring the stock to the boil in a saucepan and add the shallot and mushroom mixture. Season to taste and stir, bring back to the boil and simmer for about 10 minutes. Remove from the heat and allow to cool slightly before stirring in the cream, then serve immediately garnished with chopped chives.

Wild mushroom bisque   *Serves 6*

350g/12oz mushrooms
75g/3oz butter
1 large onion, peeled and finely chopped
575ml/1 pint vegetable stock
150ml/$^{1}/_{4}$ pint sour cream
3 teaspoons lemon juice
$^{1}/_{2}$ teaspoon salt
1 teaspoon fresh thyme, finely chopped

1 teaspoon paprika
1 teaspoon cayenne pepper
freshly-ground black pepper to taste

Fry the onion for 10 minutes in the butter, then add the chopped mushrooms together with the thyme, paprika and cayenne pepper. Cover and cook slowly for a further 10 minutes over a very low heat.

Bring the stock to the boil, then reduce the heat and simmer for 3 minutes. Pour in the mixture from the frying pan and simmer for a further 3 minutes. Remove from the heat and allow to cool, then pass through the blender. Return to the pan, add salt and pepper, and cook without boiling. Finally, add the lemon juice and sour cream, reserving a little for garnishing, and re-heat to below boiling point only, stirring all the time. When serving, swirl a little sour cream on top of each bowl.

American-style mushroom broth   *Serves 8*

225g/8oz agaric-type mushrooms
1 medium onion, peeled and thinly sliced
850ml/1½ pints beef stock
4 tablespoons red wine
50g/2oz butter
2 tablespoons lemon juice
salt and pepper to taste
croûtons

Melt the butter in a heavy frying pan and add the mushrooms, sliced or chopped, the onion and the lemon juice. Cook, covered, over a low heat, stirring occasionally, for about 15 minutes or until the mushrooms are tender.

Put the stock in a pan with the wine, bring to the boil, reduce the heat to its lowest setting and simmer for about 10 minutes. Pour the contents of the frying pan into the saucepan and continue cooking for a further 10 minutes, season to taste. To serve, pass through a sieve, discarding the solid material, and pour into individual bowls, garnished with croûtons.

Braised mushroom soup

Serves 8

225g/8oz agaric-type mushrooms
2 leeks
50g/2oz butter
1 teaspoon lemon juice
$1/2$ teaspoon salt
$1/4$ teaspoon freshly-ground black pepper
$1/4$ teaspoon paprika
850ml/$1^1/2$ pints water
1 small carton single cream
croûtons

Melt the butter in a heavy frying pan and add the white parts of the leeks, very finely sliced. Fry over a low heat until tender but not browned. Add the chopped mushrooms and continue cooking, covered, for 10 minutes or until the mushrooms are tender. Remove from the heat and allow to stand for about 10 minutes to permit the mushrooms to absorb the juices in the pan.

In another pan bring the water to the boil, then remove from the heat and add the contents of the frying pan plus the lemon juice, salt and pepper, and paprika. Stir well to mix, return the pan to the heat, and simmer for a few minutes to blend the flavours. Remove from the heat and allow to cool slightly before stirring in the cream; re-heat to just below boiling point and serve hot, topped with croûtons.

Chinese-style mushroom soup

Serves 5-6

The particular kind of Chinese mushroom normally used in this recipe do not grow wild in Britain, so you can substitute any other kind, provided that they are small and compact in shape. Dried Chinese mushrooms can be bought in Oriental food shops. A few of those, previously soaked in a little water, can be added if you have them. Include the water when adding them. Long grain rice may be substituted for noodles if preferred.

350g/³/₄lb mushrooms
2 medium onions, peeled and finely chopped
1 tablespoon oil
1.7 litre/3 pints chicken stock
50g/2oz noodles
2 dessertspoons powdered arrowroot
4 spring onions, finely chopped
salt and freshly-ground black pepper to taste

Fry the onions in the oil in a heavy frying pan for about 10 minutes. Add the mushrooms and the spring onions, both of which should be finely chopped, and cook for about 2 minutes. Pour the chicken stock into a pan with the noodles and bring to the boil, then reduce the heat immediately and simmer, uncovered, for about 25 minutes.

While this is cooking, blend the arrowroot in a small basin with 2 dessertspoons of water to a smooth cream. Pour this into the stock and stir well, bringing it back to simmering point. Add the contents of the frying pan and continue simmering for about 2 minutes. Season to taste and serve hot.

Here are various recipes for using wild mushrooms in casserole dishes, which is one of the easiest ways to use them; the long, slow cooking will ensure that they are thoroughly cooked and tender. Some varieties, of course, cook through very quickly, but a few of the more rugged kind take a little longer. I will recommend particular varieties as I go along but in some cases it matters little what kinds you use.

Mushroom casserole

Serves 6-8

225g/½lb field mushrooms or St. George's mushrooms
1 green pepper
1 red pepper
4 hard-boiled eggs
110g/4oz grated Cheddar cheese
575ml/1 pint milk, heated
75g/3oz butter

50g/2oz flour
3 tablespoons Worcester sauce
1¹/₂ teaspoons salt
freshly-ground black pepper to taste

Slice the mushrooms and fry lightly in 25g/1oz of butter. Melt the remaining butter in a heavy pan, add the flour and make a roux by stirring constantly over a very low heat. When smooth and devoid of any lumps, gradually stir in the hot milk. Keep stirring until the mixture thickens, cook for a further 2 minutes, then remove from the heat. Stir in the salt, pepper and Worcester sauce, then the mushrooms.

De-seed the peppers and remove the pith, chop the flesh into small pieces and add to the mixture. Slice the hard-boiled eggs, using a wire egg-slicer to preserve the shape. Spoon the mixture into a well-greased 2-quart casserole and arrange the sliced eggs on top. Bake in a preheated oven at 160°C/325°F (Regulo 3) for 40 minutes without a lid, and when the top is nicely browned sprinkle the grated cheese on top and return to the oven for about 5 minutes to melt the cheese.

This makes a good main course, served with a green salad and chips.

Mushroom and rice casserole   *Serves 6-8*

225g/8oz mushrooms (any of the soft fleshy kinds are suitable)
4 leeks, sliced
1 red pepper
110g/4oz Patna rice, cooked
575ml/1 pint chicken stock
110g/4oz dry breadcrumbs
50g/2oz Cheddar cheese, grated
50g/2oz butter
3 teaspoons fresh parsley, finely chopped
1 teaspoon fresh thyme, finely chopped,
1 teaspoon fresh marjoram, finely chopped
¹/₄ teaspoon ground cumin

Preheat the oven to 180°C/350°F (Regulo 4). Melt the butter in a heavy frying pan and cook the leeks over a low to medium heat until they are translucent; do not allow them to brown. When cooked, remove with a slotted spoon and set aside, leaving the butter in the pan. Chop the pepper, having removed seeds and pith, and cook in the same pan until softened. Remove with a slotted spoon and set aside, still keeping the butter in the pan. Add the mushrooms, chopped into small pieces, and cook, stirring all the time, for about 5 minutes. Yes, you've guessed correctly – these, too, should now be removed with the slotted spoon and set aside. The butter left in the pan will now be flavoured with all the juices from the vegetables.

In a saucepan, combine the rice, thyme, marjoram, cumin, parsley and stock. Cook over a low heat for about 10 minutes. Remove the solid ingredients from the liquid with a slotted spoon and layer these on the bottom of a greased 2-quart casserole dish, followed by separate layers of leeks and pepper, ending with mushrooms as the top layer.

Now pour the butter and juices from the frying pan into the chicken stock, heat gently, stir to blend, and pour over the contents of the casserole. Sprinkle the breadcrumbs on the top, followed by the grated cheese. Bake for 30 minutes, or until the cheese is brown and crusty.

Devilled mushroom casserole
Serves 5-6

The mushrooms I recommend for this substantial main dish are any of the large fleshy types such as *Tricholoma* species, but if these do not grow in your area you can use ordinary field mushrooms. *Boletus* types are not suitable for this dish.

450g/1lb mushrooms
$^1/_2$ pint water
2 tablespoons mustard powder
juice of 1 lemon
25g/1oz butter
50g/2oz dry breadcrumbs, finely ground
275ml/$^1/_2$ pint single cream
2 eggs
1 tablespoon salt
4 tablespoons chives or green spring onion tops, finely chopped
$^1/_4$ teaspoon nutmeg, grated
$^1/_4$ teaspoon cayenne pepper (optional)

$^1/_4$ teaspoon freshly-ground black pepper

Preheat oven to 180°C/350°F (Regulo 4). If the mushrooms are not too big, leave them whole, but if they are very large chop them, not too finely. Put them in a dish, sprinkle the salt and lemon juice over them and just cover with water. Put them aside to marinate for about 10 minutes.

While this is taking place, melt the butter in a frying pan, add the breadcrumbs and the chives or spring onion tops and fry over a medium heat for about 10 minutes, stirring all the time. Now remove the mushrooms from the marinade and add them to the pan, cooking for a further 10 minutes, stirring frequently.

Beat the eggs together with the cream, stir in the mustard powder, and mix thoroughly or run the mixture through a blender. Spoon the mushroom mixture into a buttered shallow casserole dish and pour the egg and cream mixture on top. Sprinkle with nutmeg, black pepper and cayenne pepper (if used). Bake for 30 minutes, without a lid, until golden brown.

Mushrooms baked in cream   *Serves 4*

This, perhaps, is not strictly speaking a casserole, but it is most easily cooked in a lidless casserole or other glassware oven dish. The mushrooms could be any of those used in the previous recipe, but in addition I recommend morels or chanterelles or both together. I do realise that these two species are less common than the others and may not grow in your area. Count yourself lucky if you find them! I certainly count myself lucky to have found morels growing in my own garden several times!

450g/1lb mushrooms
425ml/$^3/_4$ pint single cream
150ml/$^1/_4$ pint sour cream
25g/1oz butter
salt and pepper to taste

Preheat the oven to 200°C/400°F (Regulo 6). Prepare the mushrooms for cooking, leaving them whole if possible and cutting them only if they are very large. Place them in a casserole dish, and add salt and pepper to taste. Blend the cream and sour cream and pour over the top. Dot the butter on the top, and bake, uncovered, for about 15 to

20 minutes (some kinds of mushrooms may take a little longer), until cooked through. Serve with a green salad and wholemeal bread and butter.

Mushroom pasta casserole   *Serves 7-8*

This makes a very filling main course, and you can use more or less any kind of mushrooms (but see Warning on page 36!). You also have a choice as to what kind of pasta you use: macaroni, spaghetti, or the smaller varieties of other pasta shapes such as shells, wheels, twists, etc. If you use macaroni or spaghetti, either use ready-cut short lengths, or snap it into short pieces before cooking.

450g/1lb pasta
450g/1lb mushrooms
2 leeks
110g/4oz Cheddar cheese, grated
275ml/$\frac{1}{2}$ pint milk, heated
75g/3oz butter
3 tablespoons flour
2 tablespoons fresh parsley, chopped
2 tablespoons chives or green spring onion tops, finely chopped
1 wineglass medium sherry
1$\frac{1}{2}$ teaspoons salt
$\frac{1}{2}$ teaspoon freshly-ground black pepper

Preheat oven to 230°C/450°F (Regulo 8). Cook the pasta until just tender in a large pan of boiling salted water. Pour off the water and turn into a large shallow buttered casserole dish, cover with foil and set aside to keep hot.

In a 3-quart pan melt the butter and cook the mushrooms, thinly-sliced leeks (including the green parts) and the chives or green spring onion tops over a medium heat until tender. Reduce the heat to a very low setting and add the flour, salt and pepper, blending them smoothly into the mixture. Add the milk, then the sherry, and cook the mixture until thickened. The heat should be so low that although the odd bubble comes up it is not really boiling; try to avoid letting it boil. Now add the parsley and one third of the cheese, reserving the remainder. Continue to cook until the cheese has melted and blended into the mixture, aided by frequent stirring.

Remove from the heat and pour the mixture over the pasta in the oven dish, spreading the remainder of the grated cheese over the top. The mixture is, of course, cooked, so all you have to do is brown it in the oven; this will not take long. Do not cover with foil or a lid.

Casserole of ceps   *Serves 4*

This is a French recipe and is really best using the ceps which the French are so fond of. I cannot blame them, since ceps are very tasty indeed! If the ordinary common cep, *Boletus edulis*, does not grow in your area, you can use any of the edible boletus species, though the flavour may be slightly different.

225g/¹/₂lb ceps
25g/1oz butter
1 tablespoon lemon juice
4 slices of 'French stick' bread, 1¹/₄cm/¹/₂ inch thick
1 wineglass medium sherry
1 tablespoon single cream
6 tablespoons sour cream
salt and black pepper to taste
¹/₂ teaspoon paprika

The ceps should not be cut into pieces – usually they do not grow all that big. Just the caps should be used, discarding the stalks. They do not normally need peeling, but these mushrooms frequently attract débris of various kinds, which should be washed off and the caps dabbed dry with a paper towel. Examine the mushrooms carefully for parasitic creepy-crawlies, revealed by holes or burrows in the flesh, and discard any so damaged.

Cream the butter with half the lemon juice and spread this around in the bottom of a casserole or ovenproof glass dish. Next arrange the slices of bread on the bottom of the dish, and pile the ceps on top.

Sprinkle with the remaining lemon juice, salt and pepper, and pour the sour cream on top. Sprinkle the paprika lightly over the top and cover with a lid. Bake in a preheated oven for 25 to 30 minutes at 180°C/350°F or Regulo 4. Just before the end of cooking time add the sherry, together with the single cream. Do not stir these into the mixture but just swirl them on top.

Serve with creamed potatoes and glazed carrots, or a salad if preferred.

Shaggy ink cap casserole

Serves 4

The shaggy ink cap is delicious, but should be used only when very young; do not use old specimens. They must be cooked as soon as possible after picking, since they do not last more than a few hours before they start disintegrating. Strip off the shaggy 'skin' and discard the stalks.

225g/¹/₂lb shaggy ink cap mushrooms
1 medium onion
2 carrots
275ml/¹/₂ pint single cream
2 tablespoons fresh parsley, chopped
salt and pepper to taste
oil or fat for frying

Arrange the prepared mushrooms in the bottom of a well-greased casserole dish. Peel and slice the onion, and scrub the carrots and slice into thin rings. Fry the onion in a little oil or fat, and when softened put into the casserole dish and add the sliced carrots. Add the seasoning, pour the cream over the top and bake for 1¹/₂ hours in a preheated oven at 180°C/350°F or Gas Mark 4.

These mushrooms need to be cooked longer than most other varieties, but the heat can be reduced to the lowest setting towards the end of cooking time. Sprinkle with chopped parsley when cooked. This dish can be accompanied by creamed potatoes and a choice of other vegetables, or a salad if preferred.

Remember the warning about not taking any form of alcoholic drink when eating these mushrooms (see page 36).

Breakfasts

What nicer start to the day could you have than breaking your fast with a dish made with wild mushrooms fresh from the woods?

Nutritionists recommend that no one should skip breakfast, the meal that sets one up for the energy-consuming activities of the day ahead. Yet comparatively few people go to much trouble to make this meal an imaginative challenge to the taste buds. All too often they are content to dish up the same thing again and again – usually cereals, muesli or porridge followed by the traditional cooked breakfast of bacon and eggs, often with tomato, sausage and – yes – *mushrooms*. But these mushrooms are almost invariably the cultivated kind, and they are just peeled and flung into the frying pan along with the other ingredients.

The first part – the cereal course – is highly-nutritious – and should certainly not be omitted from the meal. But neither should it form the only course. So why not make the second course something to look forward to, instead of having the same dreary old dishes every day? True, it will mean that you will have to rise betimes, but is that such a heavy price to pay? The only possible problem I can envisage is that you cannot find the mushrooms you are looking for! So, although I will give my recommendations as to the best species to use in each recipe, feel free to substitute others if you have to.

Scrambled eggs with peppers and mushrooms

Serves 3-4

225g/8oz ceps
1 medium onion
3 green peppers
450g/1lb tomatoes
2 cloves garlic (optional)
6 eggs, beaten
pinch fresh basil
salt and black pepper to taste
oil or butter for cooking

Chop the onion finely, crush the garlic (if used) and trim the ceps if large by cutting into small pieces (small 'buttons' may be cooked whole). Fry in the oil or butter over a low heat until cooked through, but avoid over-browning. Remove all seeds and pith from the peppers and chop into small pieces, or thin strips if preferred. Add to the pan, continuing frying for 5 minutes.

In the meantime dip the tomatoes into boiling water to loosen the skins, remove these, and chop the tomatoes into small pieces. Put them into the pan and let them cook until pulpy, then pour in the beaten eggs and add the seasoning and basil. Continue cooking until the eggs are almost set, then remove the pan from the heat, as they will continue cooking in the heat of the pan. The eggs should be set but not rock-solid!

Baked eggs with mushrooms

Serves 2

225g/½lb large agaric mushrooms
50g/2oz Cheddar cheese, grated
4 eggs
4 slices of bread
75g/3oz oil and butter, blended
salt and pepper to taste

Pre-set the oven to 180°C/350°F (Regulo 4). Fry the bread on both sides in the oil and butter mixture. Ideally, your half pound of mushrooms should be 4 large ones. Put the fried bread slices into a greased ovenproof dish and arrange the mushrooms, with the top of the caps facing downwards (you only use the caps) one on each slice of bread. Carefully break an egg on top of each mushroom, season with salt and pepper, and sprinkle the grated cheese on top. Bake for 10 to 15 minutes or until the whites of the eggs are set.

Omelet with chanterelles   *Serves 3-4*

350g/³/₄lb chanterelles
6 eggs
salt and pepper to taste
butter for cooking
1 tablespoon milk or water
pinch of nutmeg (optional)
2 tablespoons single cream

Cook the chanterelles in butter with salt and pepper and the nutmeg if used. When the mushrooms are tender, remove the pan from the heat and stir in the cream.

Beat the eggs with the milk or water and seasoning and pour a third of this mixture into an omelet pan. Cook over a medium heat until the underside is set but still moist on top, then add a third of the mushrooms and cream, fold the omelet in half and continue cooking for one or two minutes longer, so that the filling will heat through. Make 2 or 3 more omelets in the same way.

Haddock omelet with saffron milk caps   *Serves 2*

225g/¹/₂lb saffron milk caps
4 eggs
225g/¹/₂lb smoked haddock, filleted
3 tablespoons double cream
2 tablespoons Parmesan cheese, grated
salt and pepper to taste
milk to cook haddock and mushrooms
2 tablespoons milk or water
parsley to garnish

Cook the haddock in a little milk for a few minutes, then remove from the pan and flake the flesh. Mix with the Parmesan cheese and the cream. Now cook the saffron milk caps in the milk which was used for cooking the fish, and when tender add them to the fish mixture and add seasoning.

Beat the eggs with the milk or water and seasoning, and pour half the mixture into an omelet pan. When cooked on the underside but still moist on top, add half the fish mixture, fold in half and continue cooking for one or two minutes to heat through. Make the second omelet in the same way. Fresh parsley makes an attractive garnish, and brown bread and butter can be served with the omelet.

Mushroom and bacon rolls   *Serves 6*

Large rolls are sometimes difficult to find. What I use is either a 'French stick' cut in four, or a half-baguette cut in two. Each of such portions is equivalent to one large roll.

6 large rolls
6 rashers bacon
175g/6oz small mushrooms
75g/3oz Cheddar cheese, grated
oil or butter for cooking
salt and pepper to taste

Scoop the insides out of the rolls, reserving the soft breadcrumbs. Fry the bacon in the oil or butter, then remove from the pan and chop into small pieces. Crumble the soft bread and fry the crumbs in the bacon-flavoured oil or butter. Add the mushrooms and fry until cooked. This recipe is very suitable for tiny mushrooms such as the fairy ring champignon and other diminutive species, so 2 minutes' sautéing will be enough to cook them through.

Blend the bacon, breadcrumbs and mushrooms with the grated cheese and season to taste. Dip the hallowed-out rolls in beaten egg yolk, then pile the mixture into them and place them in a hot oven (180°C/350°F/Regulo 5) for 10 minutes.

Hearty mushroom breakfast roll   *Serves 1*

50g/2oz small mushrooms
1 half-baguette
1 thick slice gammon ham
2 slices Edam or Gouda cheese
1 egg yolk, beaten
pepper and mustard to taste
fat for cooking

Spread the ham with mustard. Cut the half-baguette in half length-wise; sandwich the ham between the halves. Sprinkle with pepper. Sauté the mushrooms quickly and spread these on top of the slice of ham. Now prick the bread all over with a fork and dip in the beaten egg yolk. After leaving for a short time to enable the bread to absorb the egg yolk, pop one slice of cheese on each side of the ham. Fry over a medium heat (in the fat in which you cooked the mushrooms) for about 5 minutes on each side, until the outside is lightly browned and the cheese just slightly melting.

Kidney and mushroom sauté   *Serves 2-3*

225g/8oz lamb's kidneys
110g/4oz small mushrooms
110g/4oz butter
2 small onions
2 teaspoons fresh herbs, chopped
juice of 1 lemon
salt and pepper to taste

Slice the kidneys and remove any skin or tubes. Chop the onions into small pieces and fry lightly in the butter until soft but not browned. Now add the kidneys and continue cooking for about 3 minutes – the heat should not be too high. Add the herbs and seasoning and the lemon juice and continue cooking for a little longer. Remove from the pan and keep hot while you sauté the mushrooms in the juices left in the pan. Mix all ingredients together and serve hot with buttered toast.

Hash browns with mushrooms

Serves 5-6

My choice for this favourite American dish would be morels (if you can find them) or chanterelles, horns of plenty or shaggy ink caps. The addition of mushrooms is my own invention to make a variation on the traditional American recipe.

450g/1lb potatoes
1 medium onion
175g/6oz mushrooms
150ml/¼ pint milk
1 tablespoon oil
1 tablespoon butter
salt and pepper to taste
pinch of paprika

Peel and parboil the potatoes, then dice. Peel and slice the onion. Heat the oil and butter together in a large frying pan and cook the vegetables over a low heat for 10 to 15 minutes, stirring frequently to prevent sticking. Add seasonings and the mushrooms, cut into thin slices, and cook for a further 5 minutes or until the mushrooms are tender. Serve as an accompaniment to eggs and bacon.

Mushrooms in sour cream

Serves 3-4

450g/1lb mushrooms (any kind)
150ml/¼ pint sour cream
2 tablespoons butter
3 tablespoons Cheddar cheese, grated
salt and pepper to taste

Chop the mushrooms into large pieces; 'buttons' can be left whole. Melt the butter in a large frying pan, add the mushrooms, and season well. Cook over a medium heat for 3 or 4 minutes, stirring frequently, then add the sour cream. Stir to blend thoroughly and remove from the heat. Put the mixture in an ovenproof dish, top with cheese and place under the grill. Allow the cheese to melt before serving, perhaps with fried bread or fried potatoes.

Light lunches

The essence of a light lunch is that it should not take long to cook – or that it should perhaps not need cooking at all. An example of the latter is a salad of course. You will remember that I have stated earlier that wild mushrooms should not be eaten raw; but there is no reason why they cannot form part of a salad. All you have to do is to pre-cook the mushrooms and put them into the salad when they are cold!

Caesar salad

Serves 4

8 medium button mushrooms (any kind)
1 cos lettuce
6 tablespoons olive oil
2 tablespoons wine vinegar
6 tablespoons Parmesan cheese, grated
2 cloves garlic, crushed
dash of lemon juice
2 egg yolks
4 anchovy fillets (optional)

salt and pepper to taste
2 tablespoons butter
2 slices bread, diced

Prior to preparing the salad, lightly boil the mushrooms to cook through, then slice thinly. Sauté the diced bread in butter with garlic until crisp, to make garlic-flavoured mini-croûtons.

Now prepare the salad by combining the olive oil, wine vinegar, Parmesan cheese and seasonings in a salad bowl. Freshly-grated black pepper is best. Add the lemon juice and well-beaten egg yolks. Blend thoroughly, then add the sliced mushrooms and torn lettuce leaves. Toss all together, sprinkle croûtons on top and decorate with anchovy fillets, if used.

Mushroom kebabs   *Serves 3*

Another quick dish is mushroom kebabs. For these you will need 36 small to medium button mushrooms. I recommend ceps, but any firm kind with cup-shaped caps is suitable. The mushrooms must be very firm so that they will not open out when impaled on the skewers.

36 button mushrooms
6 tablespoons melted butter
2 tablespoons olive oil
dash of lemon juice
1 teaspoon crushed rosemary
1 clove garlic, crushed
salt and pepper to taste

Remove the stems from the mushrooms (they can be used in another dish such as a stew) and place 6 mushroom caps each on 6 metal skewers. Blend the melted butter and olive oil, season with salt, pepper, garlic and rosemary and the lemon juice, and mix well. Brush the mushrooms with this mixture, ensuring that all surfaces are coated. Place the kebabs under a medium hot grill, turning them to brown all sides evenly and basting from time to time with the mixture. The kebabs can be served accompanied by chips and grilled tomatoes.

Chicken and mushroom sauté

Serves 2-3

Button mushrooms of most kinds are suitable. The chicken and mushrooms when cooked may be piled on unbuttered toast, or served with vegetables of your choice.

450g/1lb button mushrooms
110g/4oz cooked chicken breast
4 tablespoons lard or oil
2 tablespoons white wine or sherry
1 teaspoon sugar
1/2 teaspoon cornflour
salt and pepper to taste
dash of Italian tomato paste

Cut the chicken into thin strips. Heat lard or oil and sauté the chicken strips until golden. Add the mushrooms, sliced, and stir over a medium heat for about 1 minute. Add wine or sherry, sugar, tomato paste and seasoning, cover the pan and simmer for 3 minutes.

Mix the cornflour with a little cold water to a thin cream in a basin, remove the cover from the pan, and stir into the other ingredients until the liquid is thickened, simmering over a low heat.

Spinach-stuffed mushrooms

Serves 4

The mushrooms must be big and concave enough to hold stuffing without this spilling out. I suggest young specimens of parasol mushrooms, very large ceps, field mushrooms or St. George's mushrooms. The stems should be removed and may be used elsewhere.

16 large or 24 medium mushrooms
4 shallots, finely chopped
1 clove garlic, crushed
225g/8oz cooked spinach, finely chopped
2 bay leaves, crumbled
1 teaspoon dried thyme
1 egg, beaten
4 tablespoons white wine
2 tablespoons fresh parsley, finely chopped
2 tablespoons dried breadcrumbs

salt and pepper to taste
4 tablespoons olive oil

Combine the shallots, garlic, spinach, bay leaves, thyme and beaten egg, moisten with a little of the olive oil, and season to taste. Sauté the mixture in a little more of the oil.

Fill the mushroom caps with the spinach mixture, and sprinkle with breadcrumbs and chopped parsley. Pour the remaining oil into an ovenproof dish, add the white wine and heat through on top of the cooker – an oven-to-table gratin dish is very suitable. Arrange the stuffed mushroom caps in the dish and cook in a pre-heated oven at 190°C/375°F or Regulo 5 for 20 minutes.

Eggs in a nest with mushrooms   *Serves 4*

175g/6oz small mushrooms (any kind)
675g/1¹/₂lb potatoes
50g/2oz butter
salt and pepper to taste
1 tablespoon fresh chives, chopped
4 eggs
110g/4oz streaky bacon
110g/4oz Red Leicester cheese, grated

Cook the potatoes in boiling salted water. Mash them and mix in the beaten egg yolk, butter, seasoning and chopped chives. Leave this mixture to cool slightly, then fill a piping bag fitted with a large star nozzle and pipe nest shapes into 4 round heatproof dishes.

Snip the rind off the bacon, chop into small pieces and fry in its own fat. Add the mushrooms; if some are larger than others, cut them in half, but very large ones should not be used. When cooked, place the bacon and mushroom mixture in the bottoms of the potato nests, break an egg carefully into the centre of each, and sprinkle with grated cheese. Place under a hot grill for 8 to 10 minutes, or until the egg is cooked to your liking.

Bacon and mushroom rolls   *Serves 4*

175g/6oz small mushrooms (any kind)
4 rashers streaky bacon

4 slices processed cheese
1 egg, beaten
75g/3oz dry breadcrumbs
1 tablespoon oil for cooking
25g/1oz butter

Heat the oil with the butter in a large frying pan and cook the mushrooms until tender. Larger ones should be cut into small pieces. While they are cooking, snip the rind from the bacon rashers, and when the mushrooms are cooked place a quarter of them in the middle of each rasher and wrap this round the mushrooms to form a roll. Take care that you do not put in too much filling or it will ooze out of the ends.

Dip the rolls into beaten egg and roll in the breadcrumbs. Now put them back in the pan and fry for 4 to 5 minutes on each side until crisp and golden brown. Do not let them burn! The rolls can be served with baked beans or spaghetti hoops and brown bread and butter.

Bacon and lemon stuffed mushrooms   *Serves 4*

For this recipe choose large cup-shaped mushrooms. The best kinds to use are any of the Tricholomas or field-type agarics. You should choose firm specimens – soft or flabby ones will yield poor results.

8 large mushrooms
225g/8oz back bacon
1 small onion
110g/4oz Double Gloucester cheese, grated
25g/1oz butter
1 level teaspoon French mustard
50g/2oz soft white breadcrumbs
1/2 level teaspoon dried tarragon
grated rind and juice of 1 lemon
salt and freshly-ground black pepper to taste

Remove the rind from the bacon and dice it, and the onion, as finely as possible. Melt the butter in a saucepan and cook the bacon and onion for about 5 minutes until soft but not browned.

Remove the pan from the heat, stir in all the remaining ingredients except the mushroom caps and cheese, and mix well together. Place the mushrooms with the rounded side of the cap downwards in a greased ovenproof dish and divide the filling among them. Sprinkle with the grated cheese and bake in the oven at 190°C/375°F or Regulo 5 for 15 minutes.

Ham and mushroom relish   *Serves 4*

110g/4oz ham, finely chopped
4 spring onions, thinly sliced
8 small button mushrooms (any kind)
2 level tablespoons tomato chutney
$^1/_2$ level teaspoon horseradish cream
dash of tabasco
dash of Worcester sauce
50g/2oz Red Leicester cheese, grated
4 slices bread, toasted
salt and pepper to taste

In a bowl mix the ham, onions, chutney, sauces and seasonings. Cut the toast slices diagonally and spread on the relish mixture. Pile the mushrooms on top of each half-slice and sprinkle with grated cheese. Place under a hot grill and cook until golden brown. These may be served with a green salad.

Tasty potato and mushroom cake   *Serves 4*

110g/4oz small ceps
75g/3oz butter
225g/8oz streaky bacon
675g/1$^1/_2$lb potatoes
1 medium onion
2 eggs, beaten
75g/3oz Double Gloucester cheese, grated
salt and pepper to taste

Remove the rind from the bacon and chop into small pieces, chop the onion and the mushrooms. Fry all together in some of the butter in a large frying pan for about 10 minutes until crisp and golden brown.

   Cook the potatoes in boiling salted water. Mash them, add the remaining butter, the beaten egg, seasoning, and 25g/1oz of the grated cheese. Stir in the bacon, onion and mushroom mixture, reheat the fat in the frying pan and spoon the mixture in, flattening it to form a round cake. Cook until golden brown and firm on the underside. Sprinkle the remaining cheese over the top and cook under a hot grill until the top of the cake is crisp and golden. Cut into 4 wedges and serve accompanied by a green salad.

Savoury mushroom cups   *Serves 4*

For this recipe the mushrooms should be as large as possible and cup-shaped, and they should be firm specimens. Any kind fitting this description may be used. Remove the stems of the mushrooms, discarding if tough, but if edible they may be finely chopped and mixed with the rest of the filling.

4 large mushrooms
1 can sardines in tomato sauce
1 tablespoon fresh chives, chopped
25g/1oz soft white breadcrumbs
110g/4oz Cheddar cheese, grated
1 level tablespoon grated Parmesan cheese
grated rind and juice of 1 lemon
25g/1oz butter
salt and pepper to taste
4 slices bread

Mix the sardines with their tomato sauce, chives, breadcrumbs, lemon rind and juice and seasoning to make the filling. Divide this among the mushrooms.

Toast the bread lightly on one side, then spread the other side with butter and sprinkle with grated Cheddar cheese. Place a filled mushroom on each slice, sprinkle the Parmesan cheese over the top, and cook under a medium grill for 5 minutes until golden.

Pan haggerty   *Serves 4*

110g/4oz mushrooms (any kind)
225g/8oz streaky bacon
25g/1oz dripping
450g/1lb potatoes

3 medium onions
110g/4oz Cheddar cheese, grated
salt and pepper to taste

Peel and thinly slice the potatoes and the onions, and chop the mushrooms. Snip the rind from the bacon and chop into small pieces. In a large frying pan, melt the dripping and fry the bacon for about 5 minutes. Now put alternate layers of potato, onion, mushrooms, cheese and seasoning on top of the bacon in the pan. The last layer should be grated cheese. Cover with a lid and cook gently for about 30 minutes until the potatoes, onions and mushrooms are tender, but do not stir, as the ingredients should settle together to form a kind of flat cake.

Remove the lid and brown the top under a hot grill. The haggerty is served straight from the pan accompanied by a green salad or some cold cuts.

The next two recipes can be pre-cooked and kept in the refrigerator for use the next day.

Marinated mushrooms   *Serves 4*

Ceps are best-suited, but if you cannot find these you can use agarics.

450g/1lb small button mushrooms
3 tablespoons wine vinegar
1 level teaspoon mustard powder
1 level teaspoon castor sugar
150ml/$^1/_4$ pint olive or other vegetable oil
salt and freshly-ground black pepper to taste
chopped fresh parsley for garnish

Leave the mushrooms whole. After wiping and trimming, lightly boil them for 2 minutes, and place in a serving dish. Put the vinegar into a bowl with the mustard powder, sugar and seasoning and whisk in the oil until well blended. Pour this marinade over the mushrooms, cover and leave to marinate in the fridge overnight.

When required for use, sprinkle with chopped parsley and provide some cold cuts and brown bread and butter.

Mushroom and garlic flan

Serves 4

1 prepared flan case
225g/8oz small button mushrooms (any kind)
110g/4oz cream cheese with garlic and herbs
6 tablespoons milk
2 eggs, beaten
1 level teaspoon mustard powder
2 small tomatoes

Arrange the mushrooms in the bottom of the flan case. Mix the milk, cheese, beaten eggs and mustard powder, blending well, and pour over the mushrooms. Bake at 200°C/400°F or Regulo 6 for 25 to 30 minutes or until the filling is set and golden. About 10 minutes before the end of cooking time, garnish with thinly sliced tomatoes. Flantastic!

Tasty suppers

The ideas in this chapter are for more substantial dishes which take longer to cook and will be more useful as supper dishes. Many of them can use almost any wild mushrooms, provided that you can find enough of them; a few, however, are much better using a particular type of mushroom, so in these recipes I will recommend the species to use. For the first recipe you can use either small ceps or small button agarics, or a combination of both.

Chicken and mushroom stew   *Serves 4*

225g/8oz small ceps or button mushrooms
1 medium onion
110g/4oz bacon ends
225g/8oz cold cooked chicken
425g/15oz can chicken noodle soup
2 level tablespoons tomato paste
1 teaspoon Worcester sauce

1 level tablespoon cornflour
2 tablespoons red wine
25g/1oz butter
salt and freshly-ground black pepper to taste

Snip the rind from the bacon and chop into small pieces. Chop the
cooked chicken and the onion. Melt the butter in a large frying pan,
and fry the onion and bacon for 5 minutes. Stir in the mushrooms
and chicken pieces and cook for a further 5 minutes.

Now transfer to a saucepan and add the soup, tomato paste,
Worcester sauce and seasonings. Mix the cornflour with a little water
to a smooth cream in a basin, and stir in the wine. Pour this into the
pan with the other ingredients, and bring to the boil. Reduce the heat
and stir the mixture continuously until it thickens, after which it
should be simmered for a further 15 minutes. I recommend creamed
potatoes and peas or sliced green beans to accompany this dish.

Liver, bacon and mushroom crisp   *Serves 4*

This is very tasty made with any of the smaller species such as morels,
chanterelles or saffron milk caps. If these are elusive, you could use
ceps.

75g/3oz mushrooms
1 large onion
175g/6oz bacon ends
350g/12oz lamb's or pig's liver
425g/15oz can baked beans
275ml/½ pint chicken stock
1 level tablespoon Worcester sauce
1 level teaspoon dried mixed herbs

crumble topping:
50g/2oz margarine or butter
110g/4oz plain flour
25g/1oz bacon-flavoured crisps, crushed
salt and pepper to taste

Remove rind from bacon and cut into dice. Slice the onion thinly,
and roughly chop the liver. Melt the butter in a large frying pan and
fry the onion, bacon and mushrooms for 5 minutes until soft but not

browned. Add the liver and cook for a further 3 or 4 minutes. Now transfer the mixture to a large saucepan and add all the remaining ingredients. Stir well, bring to the boil and simmer for 5 minutes.

While this is cooking, make the crumble topping. Rub the margarine or butter into the flour until the mixture resembles fine breadcrumbs. Add the seasoning and stir in the crushed crisps.

Put the first mixture into an ovenproof dish and spoon the crumble topping over it. Bake at 200°C/400°F or Regulo 6 for 20 to 25 minutes. This may be served with chips, and Brussels sprouts or another green vegetable.

Sausage and mushroom rolls   *Serves 4*

You can use more or less any mushrooms, but they should be of a kind that is easily sliced into long strips.

8 sausages (pork, beef or both)
225g/8oz mushrooms
8 thin slices white bread
2 tablespoons vegetable oil
50g/2oz butter
Dash of made-up mustard
Small quantity tomato pickle or chutney

Heat the oil in a large frying pan and cook the sausages for 10 to 15 minutes until golden brown on all sides. Cut the mushrooms into long, thin strips and cook these in the same pan during the last 5 minutes of cooking time.

Spread about half a level teaspoon of mustard and the same quantity of the pickle or chutney on each slice of bread. Remove the sausages and mushrooms from the pan and place them in the centre of the bread slices, roll them up and secure with a wooden cocktail stick at each end. Melt the butter in the pan with the remaining sausage fat and fry the rolls for 3 to 4 minutes until crisp and golden brown on both sides. Serve with bowls of hot soup.

Quick Spanish omelet with mushrooms   *Serves 4*

175g/6oz small mushrooms (any kind)
110g/4oz frozen peas

6 eggs
1 tablespoon cold water
2 medium tomatoes
8 black olives
50g/2oz butter
1 clove garlic, crushed
1 small onion
1 medium green pepper
1 level teaspoon dried oregano
salt and freshly-ground black pepper to taste

Chop the onion into small pieces and cook in the butter with the garlic in a large frying pan for about 5 minutes until soft but not browned. Remove all seeds and pith from the pepper and chop the flesh into small pieces. Add this to the mixture in the pan, together with the peas, and cook for a further 3 to 4 minutes. Beat the eggs with the water in a basin and stir into the pan with the seasoning and herbs. Cook gently until set. Add the mushrooms and fold in half. Garnish with sliced tomatoes and black olives. Cut into quarters and serve with a fresh green salad and brown bread and butter.

Beef and mushroom goulash   *Serves 4-5*

This dish should be prepared the night before you wish to use it, because the flavour is brought out more strongly after a night's refrigeration. It is best made with ceps, but if you cannot find these you can use whatever mushrooms are available (except ink caps!).

675g/1¹/₂lb stewing beef
225g/8oz ceps
1 large onion, sliced
1 clove garlic, crushed
2 tablespoons olive oil
2 level tablespoons tomato paste
225g/8oz can Italian skinless tomatoes
275ml/¹/₂ pint beef stock
150ml/¹/₄ pint red wine
2 tablespoons milk
2 level teaspoons paprika
1 level tablespoon cornflour

salt and pepper to taste
chopped fresh parsley to garnish

Cut the beef into 2½cm/1-inch cubes. In a large pan fry the onion with the garlic in the oil until soft but not browned – about 5 minutes. Add the meat and continue to fry for a further 10 minutes until evenly browned.

Now transfer to a large saucepan and add the tomato paste, paprika, seasonings, tomatoes, ceps, wine and stock. Bring to the boil, cover and then simmer on the lowest possible setting for two hours. Leave to cool, then put overnight in the fridge. If you have an electric slow-cooker, you can use this to cook it and then remove the inner earthenware or ceramic casserole dish to put into the fridge.

The following day reheat the goulash for about 15 minutes. Blend the cornflour with a little water in a basin, add the milk, and when it is the consistency of thin cream add to the goulash, stirring continuously until it thickens. After a further 5 minutes' simmering, turn out into a serving dish and garnish with parsley. The goulash may be served with boiled rice or potatoes and a green vegetable.

Creamed mushroom sauté   *Serves 4*

450g/1lb button mushrooms (any kind)
2 medium onions, finely chopped
1 clove garlic, crushed
4 tablespoons sour cream
25g/1oz butter
2 tablespoons fresh parsley, chopped
salt and freshly-ground black pepper to taste

Melt the butter in a large pan and fry the onions with the garlic for about 5 minutes until soft but not browned. Add the mushrooms and seasoning, and fry gently for 5 to 10 minutes. Stir in the sour cream and half the chopped parsley, and cook for a further 2 minutes. Turn out into a serving dish and garnish with the remaining parsley.

This can be served as an accompaniment to a joint or other meat dish with, perhaps, roast potatoes and another vegetable such as buttered parsnips or glazed carrots.

Quick mushrooms au gratin

Fry some mushrooms (any kind) in bacon or sausage fat and when cooked put them into an ovenproof dish lined with toasted or fried bread slices. Top with dry breadcrumbs and grated Cheddar cheese. Add a little sour cream, dot the top with dabs of butter, and brown in the oven at 160°C/325°F/Regulo 3.

A variation of this can be made by alternating layers of mushrooms with macaroni which as been boiled in salted water until tender. Chopped onion can also be fried with the mushrooms if liked. When cooked garnish with parsley, or sprinkle with grated cheese about 5 minutes before the end of cooking time. If you use 225g/8oz mushrooms and 110g/4oz macaroni (cooked weight) this will serve 2.

Mushroomburgers

Clean and trim any kind of mushrooms, mince them and add them to minced onions fried in hot bacon or sausage fat with herbs, chopped parsley, chives, etc. Stir well and fry until all the liquid has been absorbed.

Soak an equal quantity of bread without crusts (stale bread will do) in water until soft. Squeeze all the water out and add to the minced mushroom and onion mixture. Stir well until a crumbly consistency is obtained. Add a beaten egg and season with salt and pepper, adding a pinch of nutmeg or ground ginger if liked. Form the mixture into burger shapes, fry in hot fat and serve with chips and a salad.

We now come to some mushroom dishes which have originated in various parts of Europe. I have adapted these to avoid using mushrooms which do not grow here.

Mushrooms à la Provençale

The French use ceps more than any other kind of mushroom, and these really are the best to use for this dish.

Clean and trim the ceps and marinate them for 2 hours or so in a dressing of olive oil, wine vinegar, salt, freshly-ground black pepper, paprika and a little crushed garlic. Then fry them in hot oil with a liberal quantity of chopped fresh parsley. Serve on slices of fried bread sprinkled with lemon juice.

Funghi Fiorentino   *Serves 5-6*

This Italian dish is simplicity itself to prepare. Any kind of mushrooms may be used, but I recommend any of the large types such as Tricholomas. Firm specimens should be used.

450g/1lb mushrooms
900g/2lb tomatoes
2 tablespoons olive oil
2 cloves garlic, crushed
1 level teaspoon dried basil
pinch of marjoram
salt and pepper to taste

Quarter the tomatoes and simmer in a pan without adding any liquid. Season with salt and pepper, add the herbs, and continue cooking, crushing with a wooden spoon to reduce to pulp. When cool, pass through a sieve.

Clean and trim the mushrooms and remove the stems. If very large, cut into pieces. If the stems are edible, they may be included, cut into slices. Heat the olive oil and cook the garlic for a few minutes. Add the tomato pulp and the mushrooms, bring to the boil and simmer until the mushrooms are tender – about 35 to 40 minutes.

Funghi Napolitano   *Serves 3-4*

Another dish from Italy. The same kinds of mushrooms may be used as for the previous recipe.

450g/1lb mushrooms
2 tablespoons olive oil
2 cloves garlic, crushed
225g/½lb tomatoes, sliced
1 level teaspoon dried basil
pinch oregano
salt and pepper to taste

Clean and trim the fungi and remove the stems. As in the previous recipe, these may be used, sliced, if edible. Brown lightly in a pan with the oil, garlic and herbs. Add the sliced tomatoes and season to taste. Cook until the mushrooms are tender – about 10 to 15 minutes.

Spanish mushrooms
Serves 3-4

The mushrooms should be medium-sized – the choice is dictated by what is available. Only firm specimens should be chosen.

450g/1lb mushrooms
1 clove garlic, crushed
1 tablespoon chives, finely chopped
1 tablespoon fresh parsley, finely chopped
a little lemon juice
olive oil
salt and paprika to taste

Clean and trim the mushrooms and put them, with the stems if edible, into a dish. Sprinkle with oil, season with salt and paprika, and leave for 2 to 3 hours to marinate. Transfer the mushrooms to an ovenproof dish and brown lightly under a moderately hot grill.

Fry the garlic, chives and parsley in the oil in which the fungi have been marinated, add a little lemon juice, and pour hot over the mushrooms.

Hungarian mushrooms with paprika
Serves 2

Ceps are best for this recipe. You will need small ones.

225g/¹/₂lb small ceps
2 or 3 medium onions
olive oil for frying
1 tablespoon paprika
1 teaspoon salt
1 teaspoon pepper
150ml/¹/₄ pint vegetable stock
2 tablespoons sour cream

Chop the onions finely and fry in hot oil until lightly browned. Add the ceps whole, having removed the stems. Season with salt, pepper and paprika and add just enough vegetable stock to cover. Put a lid on the pan and simmer until the mushrooms are tender. Remove the lid and continue simmering until the liquid has evaporated. Before serving, stir in the sour cream.

Polish-style mushrooms with sour cream   *Serves 3-4*

560g/1¼lb ceps, sliced
425ml/¾ pint sour cream
75g/3oz butter
1 medium onion, chopped
1 heaped teaspoon flour
2 tablespoons milk
1 teaspoon paprika
salt and pepper to taste

Fry the onion in the butter until lightly browned. Sprinkle in the flour and stir around in the pan until the onion is more deeply browned (but avoid overdoing it!). Gradually add the milk, and keep the mixture gently bubbling. Add the mushrooms, paprika and seasonings. Add half the sour cream and simmer gently until the mushrooms are tender. Before serving, stir in the remaining sour cream.

Mushrooms au gratin Russian style   *Serves 2*

The Russians, like the Poles, the French and the Germans, seem to use ceps more often than any other kind of mushroom, although they do use other species, including several that do not grow wild in Britain. You cannot do better than use ceps for this recipe; however, you may use any kind of firm, compact-capped mushrooms if ceps are hard to come by.

450g/1lb ceps
175g/6oz Cheddar cheese, grated
3 tablespoons sour cream
2 tablespoons dry breadcrumbs
1 tablespoon fresh fennel leaves, chopped
2 tablespoons butter
2 tablespoons olive oil

1¹/₂ teaspoons flour
salt and pepper to taste

Clean the mushrooms and remove the stems, slice them and dip them in seasoned flour. Fry lightly in the oil until tender, then place in an ovenproof dish. Pour melted butter and sour cream over them, and sprinkle with grated cheese mixed with breadcrumbs and chopped fennel leaves. Brown in the oven or under a moderately hot grill.

Special mushrooms

In this section I bring together some special recipes which are really best used with one particular kind of mushroom. In just a few cases, there may be an alternative which would be acceptable.

RECIPES USING BLEWITS

Blewits and wild celery casserole
Serves 2

Either blewits or wood blewits can be used. If wild celery (*Apium graveolens*) cannot be found, ordinary celery may be used. East Anglia, where I live, is the county *par excellence* for wild celery, and it grows wild as a 'weed' in my own garden, so I do not have to plant the cultivated variety.

175g 6oz blewits
1 head wild celery

275ml/¹/₂ pint milk
25g/1oz flour
50g/2oz butter
50g/2oz Cheddar cheese, grated
40g/1¹/₂oz dry breadcrumbs
1 onion, peeled and chopped
pinch of paprika
salt and white pepper to taste

Slice the mushrooms and cook gently in the milk until tender, but do not overcook or they will become mushy, which ruins them. Remove them from the milk with a slotted spoon, and reserve the milk. Place the mushrooms in a casserole dish.

Cut the celery, including the green leafy parts, into short lengths and gently fry with the onion in the butter for 5 minutes. Blend in the flour, then add the milk in which the mushrooms were cooked. Season with salt, pepper and paprika, and pour the mixture over the mushrooms in the casserole. Sprinkle a mixture of breadcrumbs and grated Cheddar cheese over the top, and cook in the oven at 180°C/350°F or Regulo 4 without a lid, until the crumble topping is golden-brown, for about 20 minutes.

Stewed blewits

Just stew the blewits or wood blewits in milk, adding salt and pepper to taste and adding a stock cube if you want to transform the milk into 'gravy'. Cook over a moderate heat until tender, and eat with fingers of bread to dip into the 'gravy'.

It's very frustrating to have to go without this superb dish until the late autumn – blewits will not freeze, nor can one dry them.

Blewits in parsley sauce   *Serves 4*

blewits or wood blewits – enough for 4
275ml/¹/₂ pint milk
150ml/¹/₄ pint single cream
40g/1¹/₂oz butter
25g/1oz flour
4 tablespoons fresh parsley, chopped
salt and white pepper to taste

Cook the blewits, chopped into large pieces, in the milk over a low heat for about 7 minutes, then remove with a slotted spoon. Turn the heat to its lowest setting and add the cream, butter and flour, parsley and seasoning. Whisk gently with a wire whisk (not a rotary beater) while cooking until the mixture is absolutely smooth and thickened.

Now drop the blewits back into the sauce and keep over the heat just long enough for them to be reheated through. Whatever you do, the mixture must not be allowed to boil. Serve hot with toast wedges or croûtons. If you have enough blewits this makes a satisfying main dish in itself.

Blewits cooked like tripe

This Midlands recipe is slightly adapted from John Ramsbottom's *Mushrooms and Toadstools* (see 'Further Reading'.)

The stems are chopped up finely with an equal amount of onions and packed round the caps in a shallow dish with a little butter and sage. After cooking slowly for half an hour, the liquid is poured off, thickened with flour and butter, boiled and seasoned, and poured back. The whole is then stewed under cover for a further half hour and served with mashed potatoes together with apple sauce.

Creamed blewits

Slice the blewits or wood blewits and cook them very gently in a pan with enough double cream to cover them completely. Add a little salt and pepper to taste, but do not overdo the seasoning. Be sure not to let the contents of the pan boil. When tender (about 7 minutes) serve piping hot.

SOME WAYS WITH PARASOL MUSHROOMS

The young caps, while they are still cup-shaped and unopened, are ideal for stuffing. They can be stuffed with sage and onion, parsley and thyme, minced meat and herbs, sausagemeat, etc. and then arranged on a greased baking sheet (cookie tray) alternately with rolled-up stuffed bacon rashers. Cook at 150°C/300°F or Regulo 2 for about half an hour, basting occasionally with the bacon fat that exudes from the rashers. Allow 4 caps and 4 rashers per person. Parboil some potatoes, slice them across into thinnish rounds, and hash-brown them or fry them in bacon fat to accompany this dish.

Dorothy Hartley, in her book *Food in England* (see 'Further Reading') says of this species:

> Put it between two buttered saucers or soup plates, according to size, and steam over a pan, season lightly and eat with bread and butter. Do not overcook the mushroom, as its flavour is very delicate and the texture as light as a good omelet.

I would only point out that your specimens may be far too big to fit between two soup plates, never mind saucers!

She also goes on to suggest cutting parasol mushrooms into strips, tossing them in butter until cooked and piling on to hot buttered toast.

Like blewits, this species is another of our wild mushrooms that I prefer to eat cooked without other ingredients except the butter or fat used to cook them in and a little light seasoning. However, Lepiotas lend themselves to a number of 'prepared' dishes, i.e. dishes including other ingredients besides the mushrooms. Here are some recipes.

Mushroom dumplings   *Makes 8*

110g/4oz parasol mushrooms
110g/4oz self-raising flour
50g/2oz shredded suet
1 medium onion
salt and black pepper to taste
cold water to mix

Sift the flour, salt and pepper into a mixing bowl, and stir in the suet. Grate or mince the onion, chop the mushrooms (caps only) finely, and add to the mixture. Add the water a little at a time to make a dough, using the flat blade of a knife to mix. Finally knead with floured hands to make a fairly stiff dough which leaves the sides of the bowl without sticking. Divide the dough into 8 portions and roll each portion into a dumpling shape. Drop into a soup or stew about 20 minutes before the end of cooking time. Allow 2 dumplings per person.

Spaghetti with bacon and mushrooms   *Serves 4*

110g/4oz spaghetti
2 teaspoons salt
2 12¹/₂cm/5-inch parasol mushroom caps
4 rashers unsmoked back bacon
25g/1oz butter

Cook the spaghetti in boiling salted water until tender but not
mushy, about 8 minutes. Chop the bacon and mushrooms into small
pieces and fry in the butter until the bacon is crisp. Take care that the
mushrooms are not overcooked. Remove the spaghetti with a slotted
spoon and put in a serving dish. Arrange the bacon and mushrooms
on the spaghetti, and pour any remaining butter over the top.

Cabbage stuffed with wild mushrooms   *Serves 4*

Species suitable for this dish include not only the parasol mushroom
but also the tawny grisette (*Amanitopsis fulva*), the fairy ring champignon (*Marasmius oreades*), etc. You will need a lidded frying pan.

4 large savoy cabbage leaves
225g/¹/₂lb mushrooms, minced
225g/¹/₂lb potatoes
1 tablespoon minced capers or pickled nasturtium seeds
50g/2oz butter
2 tablespoons double cream
2 tablespoons chives or green spring onion tops, chopped
1 tablespoon fresh parsley, chopped
pinch coriander
pinch lovage (optional)

Boil the cabbage leaves briefly in salted water to soften. Remove
from water with slotted spoon and leave to cool. Cook the potatoes
in lightly salted water, cutting into smaller pieces if very large. When
cooked, mash with the cream and 25g/1oz of the butter. Add the
mushrooms, chives, coriander, lovage (if used) and capers.

   Divide the filling into 4 portions and put a portion in the middle
of each cabbage leaf. Wrap the leaf securely around the filling, and
skewer with a wooden (not plastic!) cocktail stick or tie with cotton
(not nylon) thread.

Heat the remaining butter in a frying pan and cook the cabbage 'parcels' over a high heat until the leaves begin to redden on all sides. Cook for a further minute after reaching this point, then reduce the heat to very low, cover the pan and continue cooking until all the liquid has been absorbed.

SOME RECIPES FOR HORSE MUSHROOMS

Mushroom ketchup

1.8 kilo/4lb horse mushrooms
4 onions
pickling spice
pinch of black pepper
cooking salt
flour for thickening

Chop the mushrooms roughly, put them in an earthenware dish and cover with a moderate amount of cooking salt. Leave for 3 days in a cool place (but not in the fridge). From time to time, turn them over with a wooden spoon.

Remove any salt remaining on top and pour the mushrooms and the liquid that has formed into an enamel pan. Bring to the boil. Chop the onions very finely or mince them and add to the boiling mixture with the pepper and some pickling spice. Stir in the flour, a little at a time, until the desired thickness is obtained. Do not use too much flour, or you will end up with a solid gooey mess!

Boil for about 20 minutes or so, and when cooked remove from the heat and leave to cool. Pass through a sieve to remove the chillies, blades of mace and other solid spices, and bottle. This ketchup will keep for 6 months or longer in a cool place, but the lid must fit tightly. Old sauce bottles with plastic screw-top lids, when washed and sterilised with boiling water, are ideal. Label with the date.

Mushroom rissoles   *Makes 8*

Try horse mushrooms in this recipe, which is very well-suited to a strongly-flavoured mushroom. As this species grows so big you will not need more than one or two.

450g/1lb mushrooms
2 onions
4 slices white bread
2 eggs
50g/2oz dry breadcrumbs
50g/2oz butter
dash of tomato purée
pinch of sage
salt and white pepper to taste

Chop the mushrooms fairly small. Soak the bread in a little water and squeeze it out like a sponge. Fry the mushrooms in the butter together with the finely chopped onions. Place in a basin together with the squeezed-out bread, beat the eggs well and add to the mixture. Add the salt, pepper, sage and tomato purée and mix well. Shape the mixture into 8 rissoles and coat them with the breadcrumbs. Fry them in the mushroom-flavoured butter left over from frying the mushrooms until golden-brown on both sides (you can add a little more butter if there is not enough).

IDEAS FOR THE GIANT PUFFBALL

The skin should be peeled off and the flesh cut into strips for frying; if desired the strips, about 1¼cm/½ inch thick, can be coated with egg and breadcrumbs, like cutlets. The strips may also be coated in batter and fried in deep fat. Little puffballs may be eaten whole cooked in this manner. Do not allow them to become darker than a light golden-yellow. Dust lightly with salt and white pepper. They make a super dish piled in the middle of an oval plate surrounded by lightly cooked chopped spinach.

Stewed puffballs in white sauce

Dorothy Hartley, in *Food in England*, gives the following recipe for small, young specimens of the giant puffball.

> Stewed puffballs, to my mind, are the most delicious fungi. The little round ones should be gently stewed in milk, till you can pierce them easily with a skewer. Then pour off the milk, and use it to make a white

sauce with butter and a dust of mace, some white pepper and salt.
Remove the puffballs to [heat] through and serve hot, with brown
bread and butter.

Puffballs in onion sauce

Dorothy Hartley goes on to give a recipe for medium-sized puffballs,
which I have very slightly adapted from her book.

Take one dozen puffballs, about the size of hens' eggs. Wipe them
carefully, and see that all are firm and white. Roll them in flour
seasoned with white pepper and salt, and drop them into a deep
earthenware pan with hardly enough milk to cover them. Add a
small bay leaf and two medium-sized onions, thinly-sliced, and
simmer gently until soft. Lift them out carefully on to a dish.
Thicken the milk in which they were cooked with butter and
cornflour, season delicately, and cook thoroughly. Pour back over
the puffs, and garnish the dish with parsley. The smooth white puffs
in their own creamy sauce, white against the vivid green parsley, look
good and taste delicious.

Richard Mabey in *Food for Free* says that a large giant puffball can be
baked whole in the oven, hollowing it out first from the bottom
where it grows out of the ground, and stuffing it with a mixture of
what he calls the 'chopped hollowings' and some minced fat meat,
preferably bacon, with some parsley and seasoning. He says the
whole should then be wrapped in foil and cooked fairly slowly – in a
slow oven, he says, though he does not say *how* slow. He admits that
he has never tried it, and neither have I. So perhaps you might be
lucky enough to find a puffball big enough to cook in this way. I
suggest 40 minutes at 150°C/300°F or Regulo 2 and see what happens.
You can always give it longer if needed.

DISHES USING MORELS

Morels have a delicious aromatic flavour and make a most welcome
addition to soups, stews, casseroles, sauces, stuffings, pies and other
savoury dishes. They are very good used in Italian risotto dishes.
They can also be cut in slices and fried, either as they are or in batter
or breadcrumbs, or they can be used as fillings for omelets and
pancakes. They are very good stuffed – being hollow they lend

themselves to this treatment better than the flat-topped type of mushroom. With all these versatile and delicious uses they could, conceivably, make your reputation as a wild mushroom cook! There is only one problem: they do take a lot of finding! Best of luck and, if you do succeed, here are some recipes.

Morels in yoghourt
Serves 2

225g/¹/₂lb morels
25g/1oz butter
4 tablespoons natural yoghourt
2 tablespoons chives or green spring onion tops, minced
¹/₂ teaspoon paprika
pinch of cardamom

Wash and dry the morels and cut them in half if they are large specimens. Grill them sufficiently to cook through. Heat the butter in a saucepan and add the chives, paprika and cardamom. Add the morels and the yoghourt and mix well. Cover the pan and leave to simmer on a very low heat for 10 to 15 minutes, stirring from time to time.

Stuffed baked morels
Serves 4

8 large morels
225g/¹/₂lb minced meat
2 medium onions
2 slices white bread
2 tablespoons fresh parsley, chopped
2 cloves garlic, crushed
salt and white pepper to taste
oil for cooking

Wash and dry the morels. Mix the minced meat with the parsley, garlic and seasoning. Chop the onions finely and add to the mixture. Squeeze the bread out in water to moisten it and mix with the other ingredients. Stuff the morels with this mixture, brush with oil and place in an oiled baking tin or dish at 150°C/300°F or Regulo 2 for 10 minutes, or a little longer if necessary.

Morels in white wine

225g/¹/₂lb morels
2 tomatoes
2 tablespoons butter
2 teaspoons fresh parsley, chopped
150ml/¹/₄ pint white wine
salt and white pepper to taste

Slice the washed and dried morels and slice the tomatoes. Fry these gently in the butter over a low heat. Add the chopped parsley and cook for a further 5 minutes, stirring all the time. Season to taste and add the wine, reheat for about 3 minutes and serve as an accompaniment to a main dish.

Creamed morels   *Serves 2*

225g/¹/₂lb morels
150ml/¹/₄ pint double cream
pinch of paprika
salt and pepper to taste

Slice the washed and dried morels. Heat the cream in a heavy pan, but on no account allow it to boil. Cook the morels in the cream, with paprika and seasonings, until soft and cooked through. This should not take longer than 10 minutes. The heat must be kept low all the time and the morels turned with a spoon from time to time. Serve piping hot with brown bread and butter.

RECIPES FOR CHANTERELLE AND HORN OF PLENTY

These two mushrooms are closely related and can be cooked in exactly the same recipes, so if you do not have the one named in the recipe, you can use the other.

Chanterelle with tomatoes   *Serves 4*

450g/1lb chanterelles

4 large tomatoes
2 medium onions
2 tablespoons single cream
1 tablespoon fresh parsley, chopped
1 tablespoon lemon juice
small quantity flour
pinch of paprika
salt and pepper to taste
oil for cooking

Chop the onions and fry in oil. Slice the tomatoes and cut the chanterelles into quarters, add to the onions and cook over a gentle heat for about 10 minutes. Season with salt, pepper and paprika, and sprinkle with flour, a little at a time, stirring continuously. Add the lemon juice and cook a little longer until the chanterelles are tender. The heat must be kept low. When ready, remove from the heat and stir in the cream, blending well. Serve sprinkled with parsley.

Chanterelle and rice patties   *Makes 24*

225g/¹/₂lb chanterelles
225g/¹/₂lb brown rice
575ml/1 pint vegetable stock
6 tablespoons Cheddar or Parmesan cheese, grated
50g/2oz butter
salt and pepper to taste
oil for cooking

Chop the chanterelles and fry in oil over a low to medium heat until cooked through, about 10 minutes. Rinse the rice and cook in the vegetable stock until tender and increased in bulk, by which time it will have absorbed most of the liquid. Cream the butter with the grated cheese in a mixing bowl, then add the cooked rice and seasonings, blending well. Add the chanterelles, having removed as much of the oil as possible.

Grease 2 12-hole bun tins and put a spoonful of the mixture in each hole. Flatten the top of each patty by pressing lightly with the back of a wooden spoon or spatula.

Bake for about 15 minutes at 160°C/325°F or Regulo 3 and serve hot with a white sauce and new potatoes, glazed carrots and spinach. This quantity makes 24 patties.

Horn of plenty sauté

225g/¹/₂lb horn of plenty mushrooms
juice of half a lemon
2 tablespoons water
¹/₂ teaspoon onion salt
1 teaspoon garlic salt
1 teaspoon ground black pepper
¹/₄ teaspoon basil
25g/1oz butter
pinch of cardamom

Wash and dry the mushrooms. Spread out in a dish and dust with onion salt, black pepper and basil, and sprinkle with lemon juice. Leave to marinate for about 15 minutes.

Heat the butter gently in a frying pan, and when a slight haze rises put in the mushrooms together with any liquid in the dish. Sauté each side for 1 minute over a medium heat if the mushrooms are young specimens, longer if they are older ones. Then reduce the heat and add the water, garlic salt and cardamom. Mix well, cover the pan and cook for a further 5 minutes. Serve hot as an accompaniment to a main dish.

THE SAFFRON MILK CAP IN COOKING

This is to my mind one of the most tasty of all our edible wild mushrooms. I'm not the only one who thinks so – the person who gave this species its scientific name called it *deliciosus*, and he was right! Its generic name of *Lactarius* means 'milk-producing' and refers to the milky 'sap' which it exudes when cut.

As mentioned on page 36, the stems should not be used, and if the mushrooms have to be chopped for cooking, do this immediately before putting them into the pot.

Saffron milk cap casserole   *Serves 2-3*

225g/¹/₂lb saffron milk caps
2 medium onions
2 tablespoons fresh soft white breadcrumbs

150ml/¹/₄ pint sour cream
1 tablespoon lemon juice
pinch of paprika
dab of butter for each mushroom
salt and black pepper to taste
oil for cooking

Place the mushrooms (caps only) in an ovenproof dish, gills uppermost, and season with salt, pepper, paprika and a sprinkling of lemon juice. Cover with a lid and cook at 180°C/350°F or Regulo 4 for about 30 minutes.

Meanwhile slice the onions and fry them in a little oil over a gentle heat until golden and soft. Remove from the oil with a slotted spoon and blend with the breadcrumbs and the sour cream. Pour the mixture over the mushrooms in the casserole dish and cook for a further 10 minutes. Put a dab of butter in the centre of each mushroom and serve with spinach and creamed potatoes.

Potato nest with saffron milk caps   *Serves 2-3*

225g/¹/₂lb saffron milk caps
450g/1lb potatoes, boiled (cooked weight)
1 medium onion, sliced
2 cloves garlic, crushed
4 tablespoons sour cream
50g/2oz butter
2 tablespoons fresh parsley, chopped
white pepper to taste
a little milk

Heat 40g/1¹/₂oz butter in a heavy frying pan and cook the onion over a gentle heat with the garlic until just soft and golden. Chop the mushrooms and add, with pepper to taste, and continue cooking over a low heat until the mushrooms are soft. Remove from the heat and stir in the sour cream.

Meanwhile mash the potatoes while still hot and cream with the remaining butter and a little milk. Make a 'nest' of the creamed potato in a large ovenproof serving dish, with a space in the middle for the mushroom mixture. Decorate the potato mixture by making ridges with a fork lengthwise on the surface.

Pour the mushroom mixture into the 'nest', and if liked place under the grill for a short time until the potato 'nest' has browned. Sprinkle with parsley before serving.

LAWYER'S WIGS IN THE KITCHEN

Before you start cooking with either this species (also called the shaggy cap or shaggy ink cap) or the closely related ink-cap, please read carefully the warning given on page 36 with regard to the dire consequences of eating either of these two mushrooms in combination with alcohol.

A recipe for the lawyer's wig or shaggy ink cap is equally suitable for use with the common ink-cap.

Lawyer's wigs in cream   *Serves 2*

8 large lawyer's wigs
275ml/^{1}/$_2$ pint double cream
salt and black pepper to taste

The mushrooms should be firm young specimens. Strip off the shaggy scales, cut in half lengthwise and arrange in a casserole dish. Sprinkle with seasoning and cover with the cream. Bake, covered with a lid, for 2 hours at 150°C/300°F or Regulo 2, by which time the cream will have clotted to form a rich, thick sauce. Serve immediately.

Stuffed shaggy caps   *Serves 2*

8 large shaggy caps
110g/^{1}/$_4$lb minced meat
1 egg yolk
2 cloves garlic, crushed
1 medium onion, finely chopped or minced
1 tablespoon fresh soft white breadcrumbs
salt and pepper to taste
dripping for cooking

Mix the minced meat, garlic, onion, breadcrumbs and seasoning, and bind with beaten egg yolk. Detach the stalks from the mushrooms, remove the scales and carefully stuff the caps with this mixture. Put the stuffed caps in a baking tin with enough dripping to ensure that the tin is well-greased to prevent burning, and roast at 160°C/325°F or Regulo 3 for about 1¼ hours or until cooked through.

These are good with chips – but the calorie-conscious may prefer boiled new potatoes sprinkled with chopped fresh parsley.

RECIPES USING BOLETUS SPECIES

For convenience the term 'ceps' will be used here to mean any boletus species, all of which can be used in the following recipes.

Cream of ceps   *Serves 2*

225g/½lb ceps
4 tablespoons natural yoghourt
4 tablespoons double cream
110g/4oz butter
2 cloves garlic, crushed
1 teaspoon salt
black pepper to taste
pinch of cayenne pepper
pinch of cumin

Steep the ceps for 24 hours in lightly salted water. Change the water two or three times; finally remove the mushrooms and rinse in plain water.

Heat about 275ml/½ pint of water, add the ceps and crushed garlic, and bring to the boil. Simmer over a medium heat until the ceps are tender. Remove them with a slotted spoon, cool and pat dry with a paper kitchen towel, and slice into strips about two inches long and half an inch wide (5cm x 1cm).

Heat the butter in a heavy frying pan and sauté the strips for 2 minutes, turning frequently so that both sides are covered. Blend the cream with the yoghourt. Now turn the heat to its lowest setting and add the cream and yoghourt mixture to the ceps. Sprinkle in the cumin, cayenne, salt and black pepper and stir well to blend all the ingredients. Then cover the pan with a lid, turn off the heat and leave for 5 minutes before serving.

Boletus stew   *Serves 5-6*

This is a good recipe in which to use all three of the edible boletus species I have described together. You can also vary the vegetables if you wish – parsnips, turnips, swedes, beans, etc. can be substituted for, or added to, the ones I have mentioned. Don't vary the quantities, though – you don't want to mask the mushroom flavour and aroma with masses of vegetables. The boletus is the thing!

450g/1lb ceps
3 medium onions
4 medium carrots
3 tomatoes, skinned and chopped
2 cloves garlic, crushed
2 tablespoons fresh parsley, chopped
3 medium potatoes
2 tablespoons flour
575ml/1 pint water
pinch of paprika
salt and black pepper to taste

Chop the mushrooms, not too small, and chop the onions roughly. Slice the carrots into thick rings and cube the potatoes into 2½cm/1-inch dice. Put the vegetables in a saucepan with the water and bring to the boil, then season with the garlic, salt, pepper and paprika. Simmer over a reduced heat until the ceps are tender and the vegetables cooked but not mushy. Try to avoid the kind of overcooking that results in the disintegration of shapes. Now add the tomatoes (if added at the start they disintegrate). Stir in the flour, a little at a time, to thicken. Finally stir in the chopped parsley, cook for a further couple of minutes, and the stew is ready.

This stew can be made more substantial by the addition of dumplings, which usually enhance any stew. In the case of this recipe, what I do is to omit the chopped parsley from the stew and mix it in with the suet dough for the dumplings instead. Drop these parsley dumplings in about 20 minutes before the end of cooking time. It is essential that suet dumplings are always thoroughly cooked.

Ceps au gratin   *Serves 4*

450g/1lb ceps, chopped
2 medium onions, chopped
1 clove garlic, crushed
2 tomatoes, skinned and sliced
2 tablespoons flour
2 tablespoons dry breadcrumbs
4 tablespoons Cheddar or Parmesan cheese, grated
125ml/4fl.oz sour cream
50ml/2fl.oz single cream
2 tablespoons fresh parsley, chopped
butter for cooking
pinch of paprika
salt and black pepper to taste

In a heavy frying pan heat some butter and put in the ceps, onions, tomatoes, garlic, paprika and seasonings. Cook over a low to medium heat, stirring frequently, until everything is golden-brown, soft and well-blended. Sprinkle with the flour and stir thoroughly to blend and thicken.

Now transfer the mixture to an ovenproof dish (no lid is needed) and cover with the combined single and sour cream. Sprinkle the mixed breadcrumbs and grated cheese on top. A few dabs of butter can be put on top if you like. Cook in a preheated oven at 150°C/300°F or Regulo 2 for about 20 minutes, or put under the grill if you prefer until the topping is golden-brown. Sprinkle with parsley to serve.

IDEAS FOR THE HONEYTUFT

Since the honeytuft does not have a very strong or pronounced flavour, far less a distinctive one, it is most suitable as a pickle.

Honeytuft pickle

675g/1½lb young honeytuft mushrooms
1.1 litre/2 pints water
175g/6oz demerara sugar
5 cloves garlic, minced
juice of 2 lemons
2 medium raw beetroots (beets), grated
4 tomatoes, sieved pulp only
2 small dried chillies
1 tablespoon salt
2 tablespoons paprika
2 tablespoons ground coriander
1 tablespoon onion salt
1 teaspoon basil
1 teaspoon ground black pepper
pinch cayenne pepper
1 large bayleaf
2 tablespoons tomato purée

Wash and dry the mushrooms. Mix the garlic, lemon juice, paprika, cayenne pepper, coriander, onion salt, basil, black pepper, bayleaf and salt. Place in a pan with the beetroot (beet), tomato pulp, tomato purée and sugar. Add the water, bring to the boil and drop in the chillies. Simmer until the liquid is reduced by half, then remove the bayleaf and the chillies. Add the mushrooms and continue simmering for about 10 minutes or until the liquid is reduced to a 'pickle' consistency. Pour into sterilised glass jars while hot, seal, cover and label. Keep refrigerated.

Honeytuft kebabs   *Serves 2*

24 medium-sized honeytuft mushrooms, caps only
4 very small new potatoes
4 small tomatoes
4 very small onions or shallots
salt and pepper to taste
pinch of nutmeg
dripping to cook

Use 4 skewers and push 6 mushroom caps, interspered with a potato, a tomato and an onion on to each skewer. Dust with salt and pepper and sprinkle sparingly with nutmeg.

Heat the dripping in a heavy, large flat frying pan (if your pan is not big enough you can use a wok, but you will need more fat). Hold the skewers with a cloth and turn them slowly round in the fat so that all the ingredients are cooked equally on all sides. When tender, serve with buttered steamed spinach or broccoli. Cooked in this way, the kebabs do not take long to do. Don't try this recipe using large, tough mushrooms, or you'll frizzle the other ingredients to death long before the mushrooms are ready.

WAYS WITH THE SPINDLE-SHANK AND VELVET-SHANK

The spindle-shank is best used in conjunction with other species in stews, soups, etc. as its flavour is too mild to be particularly distinctive. The stem is too tough to use. Young caps can also be pickled in the same way as those of the honeytuft. The velvet-shank has a stronger and more individual flavour.

These very small and thin-capped species are not really the best choice for making into the more substantial dishes described in the recipes for large agarics, but they are ideal for adding taste to an otherwise indifferent soup or stew, as a filling for pancakes, omelets and the like, or as an addition to bacon and eggs. They are also good added to a steak and kidney pie.

Preserving

Many species of wild mushrooms may be preserved in one way or another so that they will be available for use when fresh ones are not in season. They can be dried, pickled, bottled or made into ketchup; a few may be salted rather like runner beans. Freezing is not usually very successful and is not recommended.

At the end of this book I give a calendar of times at which the most important of the edible fungi appear, together with their usual habitats. This table will facilitate the collection of the particular species you want to find. If you go collecting regularly, a diary is a great help, because by making a note of when and where you find a particular species you will have a guide for the following year when going to look for it again; in time you will no doubt have memorised these times and places from your regular collecting.

It is, of course, a fallacy – one of the many popular fallacies which have attached themselves to fungi – that mushrooms can be found only in the autumn. This is simply not true. The fact is that a great variety of the larger species are most prolific in the autumn, but there are a few spring ones, many summer species, and a good many of the autumn species last right into the winter.

Just as important as knowing when to collect fungi is knowing where to look. Quite apart from the general habitat, deciduous woods, pinewoods, pastureland, etc., it is important to know something of the relationships which exist between fungi and the host which supports them. As we have seen, fungi are saprophytic, which means that they derive nourishment from dead organic matter, usually trees or other plant material, so if you know, for example, that some particular species lives on dead beech logs, then you know that you will have to look for it in beech woods. It is also helpful to know what kind of soil a species prefers because this will be the kind of soil in which the host plant grows.

Collecting fungi for preserving

Cutting fungi has some disadvantages. The cut surface of the mycelium can produce moulds which cause it to rot, and that will not do it much good if you intend to cook it. Cutting the stem of a mushroom may render identification impossible, since the formation of the base of the stem is a very important diagnostic feature, especially when identifying the dangerous *Amanita* species (see pages 9-12). One or two kinds, however, such as the honeytuft, can be cut off the substratum, and morels also can be cut. With other species it is advisable to dig them up, which will at least enable you to make sure that they do not possess one of the chief characteristics of the deadly species. Digging, as the word is normally understood, is not always necessary; most fungi can be lifted out of the earth quite easily with an old knife or a metal spatula, or even a metal spoon. In some cases you can twist the stems carefully from the soil with a slight turning movement; this is the best method with a good many species. You will be able to see the base of the stem, and you also avoid cutting, which frequently causes the mycelium to rot and thus prevents the growth of future specimens at that point. When gathering your specimens avoid bruising them, since the damaged parts quickly decay. If you have to remove the top layer of moss or leaf mould to uncover the roots of trees on which fungi are growing, be sure to replace this again, in particular the layer of material that was covering the mycelium.

It is a good idea to shorten the stem a little with a knife to see if it has been attacked by maggots inside, as this cannot always be seen from the outside. This frequently occurs with boletus species and saffron milk caps. Doing this also avoids the frustration of carrying home fungi which look perfectly sound from the outside, but when cleaned for use are discovered to be pest-ridden.

In the interests of conservation, and also to avoid killing the goose that laid the golden eggs, one should not remove all the specimens from one place, but leave one or two good-sized specimens to shed their spores; then next year you will be able to find them again. Any maggoty or overripe specimens which are no good for the pot are still able to shed their spores, so these can be usefully left *in situ*.

Do not collect fungi immediately after a long wet spell because, owing to their high water content, they will decay much more quickly. Collect on a dry day whenever possible. If collecting on a wet day is unavoidable, keep the mushrooms for only a very short time before use. Gather only young, whole specimens, but well-grown, not in the 'button' stage, because it is then that they are most likely to be confused with other, poisonous or inedible, species. Leave any which are watery, sodden-looking or burrowed by insects, soft to the touch, bruised or nibbled by mice. On your next visit you may well be able to harvest their young descendants, since the mycelium of most fungi seems to be perennial.

To bring the fungi home, place each species in a separate plastic bag and put the bags lightly, without pressure, in a shallow basket. Do not seal the bags. If, when you arrive home, you cannot prepare the mushrooms immediately – though this of course is best – keep them in a cool place (but not in a refrigerator), spread well apart so that they do not touch each other. Most species should not be kept for more than 24 hours, although a few kinds, notably ceps and parasol mushrooms, will last for two or three days in a cool place. Never wash any fungi unless they are going to be prepared immediately; the more water that gets to them the sooner they will rot.

Cleaning fungi for use

Any trimming should be done while the mushroom is absolutely dry. Grit, grass and earth can often be removed with a soft brush or, if necessary, by wiping with a damp cloth. In the case of fungi which have openings on the fruit body, such as morels, sand or grit may need to be removed from the pits. These can be rinsed quickly under a cold running tap, brushed gently, patted dry with a paper kitchen towel and folded in a cloth pending use. Any inedible parts such as scales, skin, fibrous or woody stems, the tubes of boletus species and so on should be removed.

Do not cook fungi in a metal saucepan unless you have to. If you have nothing else, once the mushrooms are cooked turn them out immediately into a china, earthenware or glass dish, and if anything is left over after the meal do not reheat but discard it.

We now come to the methods of preserving those species which are capable of this treatment. In addition to being able to use them out of season, as already mentioned, another advantage is that they are ready for use without having to go out and look for them and bring them home, clean and trim them before they can go into the pot. It is important to remember that badly-preserved fungi can easily go rotten, so ensure that the methods I am describing are carried out correctly.

Drying fungi

The easiest and probably the most popular method of preserving fungi in most countries is drying them. Many species are suited to this treatment; the kinds which are unsuitable are the soft fleshy types or those which exude a milky sap, such as the saffron milk cap. Ink-caps also cannot be used as they deliquesce quite soon after gathering.

Fungi to be prepared for drying should be cleaned carefully. Small specimens can be dried whole; large ones should be peeled if necessary and have their stalks removed. They should then be threaded on a length of string, twine or stout thread with a bodkin. A knot should be tied between each cap so that they do not touch each other; this is essential, because if air cannot circulate all around them quick drying will be impeded and mould and bacteria will invade the tissues.

When the mushrooms have been threaded they may be hung in a shady, well-ventilated place in an even temperature. Hanging them in the kitchen is not a good idea, because the steam and the changes of temperature due to cooking will affect the drying process. Steam would moisten them and cause them to go mouldy, and the changes of temperature would adversely affect the drying process. The most suitable place is a loft or attic with large windows, or an open shed which is clean and where pests such as mice or insects cannot get at the mushrooms.

Another method is to place the strings of mushrooms in baking tins and dry them slowly in a very cool oven; you could put them at the bottom of the oven which is cooling after having been used for cooking and switched off. To allow ventilation, the door of the oven should not be closed.

The third method is to place the threaded fungi on trays of wire netting (such as cake-cooling racks) or on frames covered with muslin or cheesecloth. These should be kept in the shade in a room or shed, or on a veranda where ventilation is adequate. When arranging fungi in this manner never allow them to touch each other.

A fourth method is to hang the threaded mushrooms in a large airing cupboard or, if preferred, they may be laid on the shelves. Cloth or muslin should be laid under them on the shelves first to avoid staining the wood.

Finally, a tray of fungi can be placed in front of an open fire, above a radiator, or above (not on) hot pipes.

If you are going to dry large quantities at a time, the best thing to do is to build a drying cabinet, which can also be used for the drying of fruits and vegetables. This is a portable wooden structure similar to a meat safe with perforated zinc sides and containing trays of metal mesh instead of shelves. A 20 watt bulb can be suspended from the top inside, and the whole thing plugged into the mains.

Every method of dehydration which utilises artificial heat must be used with caution, since too much heat affects the flavour of mushrooms. The time necessary to dry them for storage is difficult to assess, because it depends on so many factors: the humidity present in the air and also in the fungi themselves, the amount of air circulating, and the temperature of the immediate surroundings. When the mushrooms are in a pliable condition and show no signs of moisture they are ready. Some kinds will acquire a leathery look.

All the dry-capped types of fungi are suitable for dehydration; avoid using any kind which has a moist or sticky surface to the cap. Some kinds are especially recommended for drying; these include ceps, morels, chanterelles, horns of plenty, fairy ring champignons, honeytufts and field mushrooms. Ceps, if large, may be cut into strips lengthwise before stringing. The fairy ring champignon and other tiny species dry very quickly, being so small. If morels are particularly large, they may be cut in half.

Storage of dried fungi

Once the mushrooms are dried it is just as essential that they are properly stored as it is that they are completely dehydrated with no vestige of moisture remaining. If they are not stored in airtight containers they will reabsorb moisture from the air and then rot, or parasitic growths may attack them.

The best kind of container is an airtight glass jar with a screw-top lid. Before use sterilise the jars by boiling, dry them and warm them in the oven. Then put the dried mushrooms into the jars and seal tightly. Do not use jars with loose-fitting lids. Kilner jars with rubber rings are very good.

Reconstituting dried fungi for cooking

To reconstitute dehydrated mushrooms, just soak them in water. Some kinds – for example field mushrooms and morels – need only a few hours; as soon as they have regained their normal shape they are ready to use. Others, however, need longer; overnight is usually enough for most kinds. It is advisable to boil any reconstituted dried mushrooms lightly before adding them to cooked dishes.

Preparing powdered fungi for flavouring

This is a method of preservation mainly suitable for strong-flavoured fungi to be used in small quantities for seasoning or flavouring sauces, gravies, soups, stews, casseroles, etc. The fairy ring champignon and the honeytuft spring to mind, but others can also be used.

To prepare them, dehydrate them as already described until they are bone dry and brittle, then pound them in a mortar or grind them to a flour-like consistency in a mill or mincer. They can also be grated. Then pass through a fine sieve.

An idea for an interesting home-made flavouring is to mix powdered mushrooms with powdered herbs such as thyme, sage, etc. All these powders are best stored in small glass jars or bottles with well-fitting closures; they will keep almost indefinitely provided that the closure is airtight. I have some which I prepared eight years ago and they are as good now as they were then.

Bottling fungi

Mushrooms, particularly ceps, are bottled as a matter of course in France, Germany and other European countries. Here a pressure cooker may be used for the bottling process, but since mushrooms are more difficult to bottle than to preserve in any other way, there is some risk of all bacteria not being destroyed during the sterilisation process. It is really much safer as well as simpler to dry fungi rather than to try to bottle them.

Pickling fungi

The use of vinegar and strong spices inherent in the pickling process must be discouraged in the case of those mushrooms which have their own distinctive flavours, because the vinegar and spices tend to overpower the taste of the mushrooms. The only mushroom which is bland enough to stand this treatment is the honeytuft. A recipe for pickling this species is given on page 105.

Mushroom ketchup

The most suitable mushroom for making ketchup is the horse mushroom. A recipe for this is given on page 94.

Mushroom and tomato preserve

A preserve can be made with tomato purée and any small fungi, including ceps and field mushrooms if the specimens are small enough. Cook them in fat with a little lemon juice for a few minutes, then lift them out of the pan with a slotted spoon and pack them into jars. Take some large ripe tomatoes, dip them into boiling water to loosen the skins, remove these and cut the tomatoes into quarters. Put them into a pan with some herbs, including basil if possible, and bring to the boil, crushing with a wooden spoon (do *not* add water). Season with salt, paprika and a pinch of sugar.

Simmer over a low heat until the tomatoes are reduced to pulp, which should take about an hour. Rub through a sieve, and then pour over the mushrooms in the jars so that they are covered by the tomato purée. Close and seal the jars, and sterilise after sealing in the same way as when bottling tomatoes.

Salting mushrooms

I have no experience of using this method myself, but it is widely-used in Austria, Switzerland and Russia. The Austrians state that the mushrooms will keep for up to two years in a cool place. They claim that ceps, in particular, taste just like fresh ones collected from the woods.

Any dry-capped mushrooms can be used, but ceps, by all accounts, seem to fare best. Use large stone jars like those in which runner beans are salted, although large glass jars can also be used if you have no stone crocks. Remove any soil, grit, grass, etc., but do not wash, and trim. Very large specimens may be sliced.

Cover the bottom of the jar with a thick layer of cooking salt, then add a layer of mushrooms. Alternate layers of salt and fungi until you reach the top, ending with a thick layer of salt. Tie the mouth of the jar with three or four circles of greaseproof or waxed paper, kept in place with string or a stout rubber band. Check the jar from time to time to ensure that the fungi are completely covered, as they gradually shrink in the brine produced by the absorption of their moisture by the salt. Top up with salt if necessary and refasten the covering. A glass jar will enable you to check this without the necessity of removing the covering.

Wash the salted mushrooms thoroughly in several changes of cold water before using them in your cooking.

Calendar-guide for gathering wild edible mushrooms

The mushrooms are given in the order in which they appear in this book.

COMMON NAME	BOTANICAL NAME	USUAL HABITAT	USUAL SEASON
Blewit	*Tricholoma personatum*	Pastures, downlands	Oct.–Dec.
Wood blewit	*Tricholoma nudum*	Woods, esp. pinewoods	Oct.–Nov.
St. George's mushroom	*Tricholoma gambosum*	Pastures, downlands, esp. on chalk	April–June
Parasol mushroom	*Lepiota procera*	Woods	Sept.–Nov.
Shaggy parasol	*Lepiota rhacodes*	Woods	Sept.–Nov.
Horse mushroom	*Psalliota arvensis*	Fields	June–Nov.
Tawny grisette	*Amanitopsis fulva*	Damp woods	June–Nov.
Fairy ring champignon	*Marasmius oreades*	Downlands, parks, lawns	June–Nov.
Giant puffball	*Lycoperdon giganteum*	Meadows, grassy areas	Mar.–Nov.
Morel	*Morchella esculenta*	Wood clearings, esp. on chalk	Mar.–May
Chanterelle	*Cantharellus cibarius*	Woods	Jul.–Nov.
Horn of plenty	*Craterellus cornucopioides*	Woods, in shade	Aug.–Sept.
Saffron milk cap	*Lactarius deliciosus*	Coniferous woods	June–Dec.
Shaggy ink cap or Lawyer's wig	*Coprinus comatus*	Almost everywhere	June–Dec.
Ink-cap	*Coprinus atramentarius*	As above	June–Dec.
Edible boletus	*Boletus edulis*	Woods	May–Nov.
Rough-stalked boletus	*Boletus scaber*	Woods	June–Nov.
Orange-capped boletus	*Boletus versipellis*	Birchwoods	Aug.–Oct.
Honeytuft	*Armillaria mellea*	Woods	June–Nov.
Spindle-shank	*Collybia fusipes*	Oak and beech woods	June–Nov.
Velvet-shank	*Collybia velutipes*	Deciduous woods	Sept. to following spring
Field mushroom	*Psalliota campestris*	Fields	Mar.–Nov.

Further Reading

IDENTIFICATION OF WILD MUSHROOMS

Ministry of Agriculture and Fisheries *Edible and Poisonous Fungi*, HMSO, 1945.

Nilsson, S. and Persson, O. *The Fungi of Northern Europe*, vols. 1 and 2, Penguin, 1978.

Phillips, R. *Mushrooms*, Pan Books, 1981.

Pilát, A. and Ušák, O. *Mushrooms and Other Fungi*, Peter Nevill, 1961.

Ramsbottom, J. *Mushrooms and Toadstools*, Collins, 1953.

GENERAL READING

Beedell, S. *Pick, Cook and Brew*, Pelham Books, 1973.

Deadman, P. and Betteridge, K. *Nature's Foods*, Unicorn Books, 1973.

Hartley, D. *Food in England*, Macdonald, 1964.

Mabey, R. *Food for Free*, Collins, 1972.

Richardson, R. *Hedgerow Cookery*, Penguin, 1980.

Urquhart, J. *Food from the Wild*, David and Charles, 1978.

Also published by Green Print

The Green Cook's Encyclopedia
JANET HUNT

If you want to know practically everything there is to know about cruelty-free food and vegetarian cooking, this alphabetical handbook gives you instant information on every ingredient you can think of. There are detailed cooking hints, hundreds of recipes, historical information, and advice on buying and storage.

Plus instant guidance on such diverse subjects as barbecues, baby food, veganism, dieting and macrobiotics.

Experienced cooks will find a mine of useful information here, while newcomers to the kitchen table will welcome a book that answers all their questions . . .

ISBN 1 85425 057 4

£7.99

In stock at all good bookshops, or by post (add 60p postage) from Green Print, 10 Malden Road, London NW5 3HR.

The Scrumptious Veggie Cookbook for kids and others
MARIANNE BIRD

Milions of children and teenagers are going vegetarian. Some are cooking meals for themselves. Others are cooked for by mums and dads desperate for dishes the kids will actually enjoy!

Most vegetarian cookbooks appeal to an adult taste. *This one is different*. Pies and burgers, cakes and sweets, pasties and puddings, soups, pâtés and salads: they are all here, together with special ideas for festive occasions such as St Valentine's Day, pancake day, mother's day, father's day, Easter, Hallowe'en, bonfire night, Christmas, and New Year's Eve.

The recipes are kept simple, and are low in sugar. Meat and fish are avoided. They are all safe: older children can cook them on their own, younger ones will need some supervision. The young beginner is helped with some useful tips and a glossary. And there are no 'unusual' ingredients: everything can be found in the average supermarket or corner shop.

Finally, there's a pleasant surprise in store for the grown-ups. Although the recipes in this book have been specially created to be easy for kids to cook, and to appeal to young tastes, they also make excellent family meals popular with parents and children alike. . .

MARIANNE BIRD is a patissière whose special interest is vegetarian food that kids *and* their parents will really enjoy. She lives in Dorset.

ISBN 1 85425 058 2

£6.99

In stock at all good bookshops, or by post (add 60p postage) from Green Print, 10 Malden Road, London NW5 3HR.